THE EAST ANGLIAN and his HUMOUR

SMOKED OUT

A chimney in a semi-detached council house was on fire so the occupants sent for the local fire engine. As soon as they got into action a man and his wife, covered in soot and water, came rushing out of the other house. A fireman calmed them down:

'you don't want to worry yourselves a mite. That ain't your chimney on fire. We just put the spout down the wrong chimney.'– *George Webb, Boxford, Suffolk.*

BLOODSPORTS

Overheard at a local meet of the Suffolk foxhounds:

'I don't agree with this ode sport. It ain't roight they keep mardling about all over the filds. If I had moi way it 'ouldn't be allowed.'

(Some deliberation).

'Poor ode hosses.'– *P.J. Tebbitt, The Wick, Boxted, Suffolk.*

HOW TO STRIKE A MATCH

An old yokel purchased a box of matches from a village shop but when he reached home two miles away he found the matches wouldn't strike on the box as it was damp.

Back he trudged to the shop and in a loud voice exclaimed: 'Here! These duzzy matches won't strike, mister.'

The shopkeeper took the box from the yokel, withdrew one of the matches and, lifting up his leg to make the seat of his trousers tight, struck the match on his hindquarters.

'There,'he says. 'That's all yew gotta dew.

The old yokel looked, scratched his head.

'Well, bor,' he said, 'if yew think Oi'm a-comin' tew moiles to strike a match on your starn, yew made a great mistake.'
– Mrs. O. M. Carpenter, 94 Greenfield Avenue, Eastfield Estate, Northampton.

HE DOAN'T FRIT ME

The following conversation took place between myself and a secondary modern school pupil recently:

Master (to boy who jumps to other side of desk when books are being inspected): 'Why do you jump like that?'

Pupil: 'You frit me, sir,'

Master: 'Frit! You don't say that to your English master, do you?'

Pupil: 'Naow! He doan't frit me!'
– Anthony Beaumont, 'Waynefleet,' South Wootton, King's Lynn.

THE SWINE AND THE BACON

Judge Bacon, who, many years was on the Norfolk circuit, once had before him a man named Swine. The judge, in the course of the case, jokingly remarked:

'You know, my friend, the devil entered into the herd of Swine.'

'Yes, my lord,' replied the defendant. 'And remained in the Bacon to this day.'
– J.F.R. Buttle, Turret Cottage, Lynton, Devon.

LATE BACK

Over 40 years ago, in the Norfolk village where I used to live, Tom had been on a day's outing to Great Yarmouth. He arrived home very late and in an inebriated condition.

His wife was waiting up for him and as soon as he staggered into the house she asked:

'Wherever hev yew bin all this time?'

'Yarmouth,' replied Tom.

I'll give yew Yarmouth,' said the old lady. 'If yew can't git in sfore this hour, the next time yew go tew Yarmouth yew stop at hoom.' *– Mrs. I. Turner, 71 Crossroads, Elvedon, Thetford.*

THE SUCCESSFUL MILLER

Heard at the hollesley field day sports. As the girls were lining up for their race a resident said to a visitor:

'I bet you a tanner a Miller girl will win this race.'

The visitor asked him which one of the girls was Miss Miller and the resident replied:

'They're all Millers.' *– C.K. Eldridge, 81 Grundisburgh Road, Woodbridge.*

ONE–WAY TRAFFIC

One old boy talking to his neighbour over the fence:

'Dew yew know, bor, some of your owd chickens come into moi back yard?'

'Cos I dew!'

'How dew yew know?'

'Cos some of the ––––s don't come back!' *– Jack Eggett, 151 Valley Road, Ipswich.*

Drawing by Jean Creswell

WASTING TIME

A Suffolk parson had some glebe land he required ploughing and he hired a neighbouring farmer's horseman and team to do the work. Watching, the parson noticed that the horseman stopped for some time at the end of each furrow, so the asked the reason for this apparent waste of time.

'Must wind the hosses, parson, must wind the hosses,' was the reply.

The parson went away, returned with a hedging tool and said:

'While the horses are getting their wind, John, you might cut the hedge for me.'

John was somewhat taken aback and said:

'Parson, you know that although we have a large family and there is a lot of housework to do, my missus and me come to church every Sunday?'

'Yes, I know, John,' the parson answered, 'and very pleased I am to see you.'

'Well,' said John, 'how would it be if next Sunday I brought a stone of taters in a bowl and you peeled 'em toime we're singing the hymns?' – *G.H. Welch, Manor Farmhouse, Saxtead Green, Woodbridge, Suffolk.*

THE CLOCK THAT WOULDN'T GO

Arriving home from work one night Tom was told that the clock had stopped so after tea he tried to mend it. After much effort he still couldn't get it to work and finally he found a dead beetle inside.

'No wonder the old clock stopped,' said Tom. 'The old engine driver's dead.' – *Frank Reece, Freckenham, Nr. Bury St. Edmunds.*

LOST AND FOUND

During the war, when it was an offence to possess corn acquired otherwise than by official allocation, someone I knew was given a sack of wheat by a customer in East Anglia. He put it in the back of his car to take home for his chickens.

On the way home he was stopped by a police road check, who asked him what was in the sack. Extempore, he replied that it had dropped on to the road from a lorry he had been following and that he was about to take it to a police station. He then had no option but to take it there and deposit it as found property.

Some months later he was in the district again and decided to claim the corn, knowing that no one else could properly have done so. The sergeant at the police station instantly and unblushingly told him that the corn had been claimed by the owner within a week of deposit.

There was nothing further to be said but, as my friend walked sadly down the path from the police station, his eyes were caught by the sergeant's plump chickens strutting round their run.

J.B. Tyrer, April Cottage, Fulborn, Cambridge.

Drawing by Jennifer Kent

VERY NEARLY ALL

At the harvest festival held in a Suffolk village the local wits used to sing:

'All is safely gathered in—

Except Charlie Fordham's, which is late agin.'

– Miss B. Howard, 11, Chester Road, Felixstowe.

FAIR ENOUGH

The farm foreman went to see one of his workmen and said:

'George, you lost two days last week.'

'I know,' said George. 'I'm going to make that up Saturday afternoon.'

– C.E. Grainger, Hoveton Fruit Farm, Hoveton, Wroxham, Norwich.

WHOA!

During the scripture lesson in a Norfolk village school a small girl was asked to describe in her own way the passage from Genesis dealing with Abraham's sacrifice of his son Issac. This she did and told how Abraham bound Isaac and placed him on the altar and raised his knife to slay his son when 'God hollered out: "Whoa on there, yar gorn far enough".

L.T. Huggins, 85 Florence Road, Maidstone, Kent.

NO LAUGHING MATTER

Old Albert went to work one mourning with a bandage round his neck.

'Wass amiss with yar neck?" asked the farmer.

'I a-got a grut owd push on 't' replied Albert.

'That hut 'e, I 'spect, don't it?. said the farmer.

'Well, marster,' said Albert, 'if you can keep from howlin' that'll keep you from larfin'. – *C. Woolnough, 8 Woodville Road, Ipswich.*

SUCCESSFUL CAMOUFLAGE

During the early days of the last war attention was called by high authority to the council houses (one of which I inhabited at the time) on the ground that they were a mark for invading aircraft. So they were duly camouflaged and the outer walls reduced to quite a mixture of colours. A caller, noticing the effect, remarked:

'How gay they look now!'

To which my neighbour promptly replied:

'Yes don't they. There aren't one aloike.'— *E.M.M. Martin, Eastview, Stoke Road, Clare, Suffolk.*

THE REASON

Here is a story my step-mother told me. (She was born in 1834 so it should be getting ripe now).

Two old cronies had not seen each other for some time and when they met, after the customary howdoes. Alfred enquired after James' wife. A pause followed and then:

'James, you dinn't ask me how my wife was.'

'No, Do you know why?'

'No,'

'Well, I didn't wanter know.'

— *G. Bloomfield, 47 Cliff Lane, Ipswich.*

BURIAL OF A GIANT

It was after the death of the last of the Hales family of Somerton, noted for their great stature. The man who had been buried that day was over seven feet tall and the matter was being discussed the same evening in the local. A stranger who happened to be present was very sceptical and 'mine host' was appealed to settle the argument. He said, very decidedly:

'Of course he was as tall as they say. He must have been because when it came to the funeral the coffin was so long they had to make two journeys of it.' — *Mrs. Cicely M. Fathers, 100 Upper Cliff Road, Gorleston-onSea, Norfolk.*

WAIT FOR THE FUNERAL

An old fellow was ill in bed and had not been allowed anything to eat for several days. One day the doctor called and told the wife her husband wouldn't last much longer and he could have anything he liked to eat. After the doctor had gone the old woman called up the stairs:

'The doctor say you can hev anything yow like to eat,' and the old man called back with delight:

'Cord, I'd like some o' that there ham yow a got cooken down there!'

To which came the sharp retort:

'Yow can't ha' that. Tha's for the funeral.' — *F.G.G. Cobb, 29 St. William's Way, Norwich.*

CAN YOU SOLVE THIS, TOGETHER?

What is it? A man made suffen he didn't wornt. He sowd it to a man that couldn't yewse it. And the man that had ut didn't know he'd got ut.

Answer: A cawfin. — A.J. Nunn, Eldernell, Gt. Blakenham, Suffolk.

TONGUE TWISTER

'I say, bor, they say thut I say "I say" afore ev'ry word I say an' if I do say "I say" afore ev'ry word I say thus no reason why they should say I say "I say" afore ev'ry word I say, so there, I say, bor.'

—*Mrs. R. Clover, Buxhall Mills, Suffolk.*

WHAT THE CHURCH BELL TOLLED

The rustics in the bar-parlour left untouched the ale in their tankards as they quietly counted the strokes of the passing-bell from nearby St. Mary's Church.

As the echoes of the last solemn note died away the youngster of the party broke the silence.

'Seventy-two.' he said. 'I wonder who that's for, dad?'

'Dunno, bor,' said the old un. 'But there's one thing I do know. It's for nobody who live in Woodbridge.'

—Ernest S. Willott, Derby House, Woodbridge.

THE NON-RETURN OF MRS. G.

My farther used to tell this story which he said concerned the Rev. Banks and a character in the Trimley district.

The character was Mr. Giles, a farmer, who had a very jealous wife. As she lay dying Mrs. G. threatened her husband that if he married again she would 'scrab' her way out of the ground and haunt him always.

However, a few years after her death Giles did marry again and the parson, who had been present when Mrs. G. had made her threat, asked Giles if the memory of the incident disturbed him in any way.

'Whoi bless yew, parson,' said Giles.

'Don't yew know? I buried owd Hannah face down, so the harder she scrab the fudder down she keep a-going'.

— H.B. Kidd, P.O. Box 248, Ajax, Ontario, Canada.

WHEN THE TIDE COMES UP

Two elderly farm workers were persuaded to join the village choir outing to the seaside. They went by train and took their 'wittals' (bottles of cold tea and bread and cheese) with them.

Coming back, Billy noticed some clear liquid in Jimmy's bottle and the following conservation ensued:

'What 'a ya got in yar bottle, Jimma?'

'Sea watta, Billa.'

'What a ya gorn a du wit?'

'Billa, bor, I'm a-gorn a taake it home an'show my old missus. She hen't never sin the sea.'

'You'll never git that home, Jimma,'

'Why on't a?'

'Cos you on't yu fule yu. When the tide cum up that'll bust that there bottle.'

— Ernest H. Knights, Foundry House, Harleston, Norfolk.

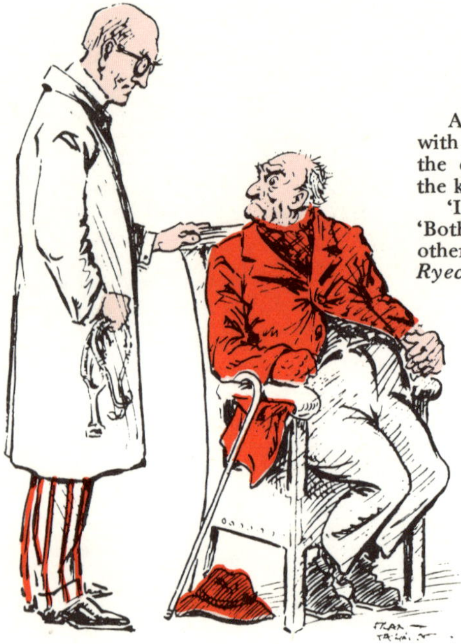

BOTH ALIKE

An old man went to see the doctor with knee trouble. After examination, the doctor said he thought the pain in the knee was due to old age.

'I shan't have that,' said the old man. 'Both my knees are the same age and the other one's all right.'– *J. Maynard, Ryecroft, Whittlesford, Cambs.*

Drawing by Frank Harrison

THE RIGHT TIME

This true experience befell my father on his travels in Suffolk during the war. It was mid morning and he stopped to ask the time of a farm labourer who was engaged in muck spreading.

After gazing up and down the field for some moments, the labourer leant on his fork and said:

'Well, bor, when Oi've spread another four rows o' muck, Oi reckon that'll be 'bout a quarter arter twelve.'

I have no doubt that it would have been.
– B.E. Weller, 405 Bradford Apts., 3301 St. Paul St., Baltimore 18, Md.,' U.S.A.

CATECHISM

Our rector was preparing a class for Confirmation and one Sunday he was questioning them on their knowledge of the catechism. He asked one girl:

'What is your name?'

'Molly Slop Shoes.'

'Who gave you this name?'

And instead of answering 'My Godfathers and Godmothers in my Baptism,' she replied:

'Bob, the butcher boy, and Mother says when she sees him she'll slap his chops.' – *Mrs. J.H. Wallace, Ford Hall, Long Melford.*

GUARANTEED

In a chemist's shop a lady was asking for the hardest tablet of bath soap available, as her twin daughters played with the soap so much in the bath that it shrank quickly. When the choice had been made the assistant wrapped the soap and handed it to the customer saying:

'If it doesn't last, you must bring it back!' — *Mary K. Mills, 39 Garrison Lane, Felixstowe.*

Drawing by Paul Hogarth

WHAT A SIGHT

A countryman went to have his eyes tested. When he came home he said:

'They took both eyes out and laid them on the table. I never see such a sight in all my born days.'
— *W.G. Munnings, The Rookery, Weybread, Diss.*

LENGTH OF RESIDENCE

An Essex countryman, applying for some benefit or other under some scheme or other of the welfare state, filled in a long form and posted it to the appropriate government department.

It was returned to him for correction and he could not understand why.

It transpired that in answering the question 'Length of residence in Britain' he had written '45 feet' (the distance from the front to the back of the house in which he lived).
— *J.H. Burton, 22 Esplanade Gardens, Westcliffe-on-Sea.*

SILENCE IS GOLDEN

Scene: Cottage living room, lighted by oil lamp. Mary Ann is making herself a new dress, husband sits watching. Mary Ann holds up material which she has cut through table cloth as well.

Mary Ann: 'Oh, Walter, look what I've bin and done.'

Walter: 'Well, I've bin watchin' yer and I've bin thinking to myself if yew aren't a-cuttin' through that table cloth thass a rummun to me.'
— *Mrs. W. Baker, Decoy House, Nacton, Ipswich.*

NOT GUILTY

On being summoned to sttend a London Petty Sessions for a speeding offence recently a local farmer wrote the following letter to the justices to explain his inability to attend.
–Mrs. Ronah Rhodes, Stone Street Farm, Hadleigh.

As yew know Charlie lef me lars week on account of his missus wanten to goo an live near Ipswich an the pitchers an owd Fred he wholly got set in the back arter runnen about in the cowd arter they fireworks. Yew know that wor wholly damp down on the low midda, so o course he ent much cop at getten the beet up an Mister Brown what cart my beet he don't half carry on if I won't use me permits when he say, so yew see I can't git up Lunnen for this here business for reasons aforestated.

Howsumever, as me owd Aunt Jessie used to say, I trust your honour will not be too hard on me seeun as how I never knew about gorn more un 30 in me truck cos the bloke I bought it orf he say yew can goo as fast as yew loike bor, he say, an he oughta know seeun as how he a got one o they cars with a ingine in the back. Well, he say, this here pick-up truck is wholly handy cos yew can goo to Colchester with a coupla ole sows and the missus as well an she oont keep createn an sayen this here van wholly stink loike she did about the lars one I had. So yer see thas how it is and I thowt that were a car at the front an a lorry at the back an I hadn't got any sows in when they coppers pulled me up, owny me missus, so if yew loike I reckon as how I could send yew a coupla brace o pheasants nex week an we'll ferget all about it.

SMALL FOR ITS AGE

My brother Tom was stable boy to Farmers Bouce at Chilver House Farm, Leziate, and after every market day at King's Lynn the agent to old Squire Hammond of West Acre, Mr. Friar, would call and spend the evening.

When he was ready to leave, Tom would take his saddle horse round to the front door. On one occasion the visitor slipped a silver threepenny bit into Tom's hand. Tom held it down to the latern and examined it closely.

'What's wrong with it, Tom?' saked Mr. Friar. 'Ain't it a good one?'

'I was looking for the date,' replied Tom.

'What has the date got to do with it?' asked the visitor.

Tom replied: 'I thought it was very small for its age.'– *J.F.R. Buttle, Turret Cottage, Lynton, Devon.*

THE SAFEST PLACE

A Norfolk farm worker who lived in a bungalow was in the habit of putting a basin of bread and milk on the side of a low brick stove to keep worm for his early morning breakfast. One night his wife thought she heard the plate covering the basin move.

'Will, Will,' she said, rousing him, 'I now heerd yar plaat slip orf the baasin. The sut'll git interyar bread an' milk.'

'All right,' said Will, getting out of bed, 'I'll sune alter that.'

He was gone a considerable time and on his return his wife asked:

'Where'd yew put it, Will?'

'Where the sut can't git into it,' answered Will. 'I eart it.'–K.C. *Ford, 5 Golden Dog Lane, Norwich.*

DINNER FOR SATAN

A parson was going round the village delivering his magazines and unfortunately let them fall on to the muddy road. He picked them up and put them into a hnadkerchief to carry, tying the corners into a knot.

On his way he came to some workmen with the road up and one of them was using strong language. The parson went up to him and said:

'My man, do you know Satan?'

'No, 'said the man. And then, shouting down to his mate: 'George, do you know Satan?'

'No, bor. Why?' was the reply.

'Well there's a bloke here brought his dinner.' – *Launcelot Sanderson, The Firs, St. Lawrence, Nr. Beccles.*

A SAD STORY

A dear old lady in the village was reading the story of the crucifixtion to another old lady who couldn't read. When she had finished the listener said:

'Lor', my dear, thet dew fare sad.'

'Yis,' said the reader as they both dried their eyes, 'let's hoop thet worn't trew.' – *Mrs. G. Goddard, 67 Springfield Lane, Ipswich.*

BLACK HEN EGGS

The village character went into the shop and asked for a dozen black hen eggs. The shopkeeper, somewhat taken aback, asked him what he meant and he repeated the order. Of course, she had never heard of such things and said so, adding that if he knew a black hen's egg when he saw one he could pick out a dozen.

Selecting 12 of the biggest in the container he said: 'There yew are, ma'am. These are black hen eggs.' – *George Bloomfield, 47 Cliff Lane, Ipswich.*

NO CASTOR OIL

During the war some Cockney children were evacuated to an East Anglian farm. They had rabbit served up for them in various ways the whole week and on Sunday the farmer said:

'I know you've not been used to eating all this good food, so I'd like you all to take a dose of castor oil as we at the farm do.'

'I don't want any!' exclaimed one little boy defiantly.

'Why not?' asked the farmer. 'It will do you good.'

'I don't want any castor oil. All I want is a ferret.' – *Mrs. V. Chipperfield, 44 Commodore Road, Oulton Broad, Lowestoft.*

SPARE TIME

In the days before radio, Carlton Hall near Saxmundham boasted a fine clock whose chimes set the time over a wide area. The coachman at the hall used to ride on horseback to Saxmundham to post letters and one night he left the hall at five minutes to eight by the clock and on arriving at the post office observed that the clock there showed seven minutes to eight. To the bystanders he remarked:

'This sartinly do be a rare foine mare. We ha' got here in no toime and had two minutes to spare.' – *A.E. Orford, 7 St. Mary's Crescent, Felixstowe.*

LEARNING ABOUT SIN

New vicar (who had brightened up village life with socials, concerts, outings):

'You must have noticed a difference since I arrived, Mrs Smith?'

Mrs Smith: 'That we have, vicar. Why bless you, sir, we didn't even know what sin was till you came.'

– *S. Lummis, 32 High Street, Ipswich.*

CANDOUR

Two old countrywomen met outside my shop one day and I overheard the following conversation:

'Hallo, Mrs. Brown. I ain't sin yer for a long time. 'Ow are yer?'

'Oh,' replied the other, 'I ain't very grand. I don't feel wuth a ha'penny.'

'No,' said her friend, 'an' yer doan't look it.'

– H.W. Marchant, 6 Withersfield Road, Haverhill.

CYCLISTS AND PRESBYTERIANS

My father wanted to know where the cyclists' entrance was at the Suffolk Show and he asked his mate to find out. Next day his mate reported:

'Yew take the farst tarnin' on the roight before yew git tew the show. There's a notice that say: "Motor cyclists and Presbyterians." '

My father replied: 'Where do the Church of England go?'

To this his mate said: 'Are yew trying to take the micky out of me?' *– Elizabeth Garnham, (aged 14), Church Road, Old Felixstowe.*

ON THE SAFE SIDE

'Mrs. Brown,' said the parson after the service, I notice that you quite correctly bend the knee when the name of our Saviour is mentioned. I also notice that you bend the knee when the name of the evil one is mentioned. Will you tell me why?'

'Sartainly,' said Mrs. Brown. 'It cost you nawthen to be polite and you never know.' – *M.I. Harrison, Gun Hill Cottage, Southwold.*

SATINWOOD

A master at Harkstead School, near Ipswich, was giving a class a lecture, many years ago, on the different types of English woods and their uses in the making of pieces of furniture such as tables, chests-of-drawers, etc.

At one point during the lecture he asked young George the kind of drawers most common in his mother's house.

The boy, with a hard thinking look on his face, spluttered out:

'P-p-p-pink flannelette, Sir.'

– *D.C. Nevin, Caixa Postal 571, Rio de Janeiro.*

WARNING

Some years ago, when boys could get permission to leave school for special purposes an inspector visited a school near Fakenham. The boys were asked what work they intended to do if they got permission to leave.

One boy said he was going to 'oller 'old ye. H.M.I. was was quite unequal to this language and asked what was meant. No one could explain until a 'local' teacher was brought who said it meant that he would lead the horse and cart in the field at hay time and shout 'hold you' to the man on the load when the horse was about to go forward.

– *H. Driver, 243 Upper Grosvenor Road, Tunbridge Wells.*

A GOOD FRIEND

My grandfather (who was a clergyman) was visiting one day and remarked to a woman in the village that she had had a very large family. Much to his amazement she replied. cheerily:

'Yes Sir. Thas roight. An' if the churchyard ha'nt have been a good friend to me, I don't know what I should have done.'

– *Miss Alison M. Fraser, Weston Hall, Weston, near Beccles.*

A HAPPIER PLACE

'This would be a sad world,' remarked an old Suffolk countrywoman, 'if it were not for the blessed hope of immorality in the next.'

– *From 'Memories of a School Inspector' by A.J. Swinburne.*

BACKING UP

Many years ago, my grandfather was looking round an old cottage with a view to purchase. The tenant at the time was a very stout man and my father, noticing how small the privy was, remarked that he must find it hard to turn round in such a small place.

The old man's reply was:

'Lor', I don't turn round in there. I undoes my braces outside and backs in.'

– *J. Maynard, Ryecroft, Whittlesford, Cambs.*

CHEAP RATIONS

An old neighbour of ours in south Norfolk who always went in for pigs was roused one morning by his yard boy who said:

'Marster, you'd best come down. That owd sow is atin' her pigs.'

'Thass all right, bor,' said the farmer. 'She can't eat anythin' cheaper.'

– R.H. Futter, Thwaite St. Mary, Nr. Bungay, Suffolk.

THE ROSE OF SHARON

In a suffolk village school a little girl named Rose had around her a most unclean odour. The teacher could stand it no longer so wrote a polite note to the girl's mother. Come the reply:

'My Rose ain't no blooming rose for you to larn her not smell her. – Mrs. Blank.'

Ever after that she was called the Rose of Sharon.

– Mrs. L.J. Durrant, 117 Spring Grove Crescent, Hounslow, Middx.

HOBGOBLINS

Shortly after a jet aircraft crashed near Levington a helicopter flew to the scene to pick up the pilot from the river.

An ancient local inhabitant was heard to mutter to himself: 'Tha's a rummon to me how them hobgoblins pick fooks up.'

– E. Felgate, Oak House, Bucklesham Road, Nacton, Ipswich.

THE FIRST VEIL

I remember a young woman from Lammas going to London as a domestic servant and, after a time, home she came 'cracking her jaw' as they called it.

On Sunday morning she was in Lammas church with a veil on. She had bought it in London but this was the first time she had worn it and she blew her nose through it.

– A. Parnell, Bear's Grove, Salthouse, Norwich.

SELF DEFENCE

Going home from school one day Big Brother found Sister Bessie in tears.

'Well, there, mor, whatever are yew bla'ing about?'

It's owd Cissie Podd – she give me a clout.'

'Whur, gal, stop your hollerin', dew. Yew dew what I dew – hit back fust.'

– Mrs. W. Baker, Decoy House, Nacton, Ipswich.

A NEAR THING

Two dear old ladies living near here used to creep round the lanes in an ancient Chevrolet with a very high chassis. One day, on turning a corner, they ran clean over the local roadman, who was leaning on his shovel.

One of them looked out of the back window of the car and said:

'My dear, he's underneath. You're on top of him.'

The other immediately put the car into reverse but by that time the man had got up on his knees and they ran over him again.

Some years afterwards someone said to him:

'Do you remember the day you got run over twice?'

'My word, yes', he replied. 'That was a nie 'un, worn't it?'

– George Webb, Boxford, Suffolk.

PROPOSAL

Sarah, a valued maid in our family for 30 years, had several proposals in her life but she remained single to the end.

One yokel, evidently very shy, wrote: 'Dear Sarah: If I walk along wi'yow, will yow walk along wi' me? My mother towd me to arsk yer. Jimmy.'

– *Mrs. R. Clover, Buxhall Mills, Stowmarket.*

BUSINESS IS BUSINESS

More years ago than I care to remember I was serving articles to a firm of Norwich solicitors and used to travel from Sheringham to Norwich daily by train. One market day several farmers were in the carriage and at a later station there entered a most respectable and prosperous-looking gentleman. He wore a hard felt hat, neatly trimmed grey beard, a grey suit, fawn leggings and a heavy gold watch chain. He was greeted with respectful 'good mornings' by all except one of the younger men who said:

'Yew owd rascal. I a-got a bone to pick wi' you!'

'Why, what's the matter wi' you?'

'That mare yew sold me. Quiet to ride and drive, yew said, dint yer?'

Yes and so she were.'

'Fit for a lady to drive, yew said, dint yer? A good thing I didn't let my old missus drive on't.'

'Well, what's the trouble?'

'Trouble! Only that the mare is shot, the trap is smashed and I a-bin three months in horspital. I reckon an owld gentleman like yew should a-known better.'

At this the old man burst into cackles of laughter and when his mirth had subsided he said:

'Well, if yew a-got something to sell yew don't go a-crying stinkin' fish, dew yer?'

– *W.R. Kempson. 'Kay Wick', Chincilla, Queensland, Australia.*

WELL INFORMED

Overheard outside my office window when the Duke of Edinburgh visited Ipswich on 1 May, 1956:

'What's all the flags out for, bor?'

'The dook's in the town.'

'What's he a-doin' of?'

'I don't rightly know, mate!'

– *H.N. Collinson, 8 Princes Street, Ipswich.*

BROAD HINT

The Verger took the visitor round the church and expounded his knowledge of its history and architecture. After a lengthy stay the visitor was leaving without giving a tip and when about 20 yards away heard the verger call out:

'Excuse me, sir, but when yew git home, if yew foind you've lorst your purse, yew didn't take it out here.'

– *Wm. Dent, 7 Copleston Road, Ipswich.*

M.P.H.

A hiker on his way to Lowestoft passed through Blundeston and, being in rather a hurry, asked a yokel who was hoeing his garden:

'How long will it take me to walk to Lowestoft?'

'Couldn't tell yer,'said the man.

'Oh, well, thanks all the same,'said the hiker and walked on.

He was about 100 yards along the road when, hearing a shout, he turned to see the yokel leaning over the gate and beckoning to him. Puffing a bit the hiker retraced his steps and asked:

'What's the matter?'

'Well,' said the yokel, 'it'll take you about an hour and five minutes to walk to Lowestoft.'

'Thanks,' said the hiker. 'But why the Dickens didn't you tell me that before?'

'Ah!' said the other. 'I din't know how fast you was a-walking.'

– *R.A. Rose, 1 White Horse Street, Lowestoft.*

GOOD MANNERS

Many years ago a certain gentleman in Eye gave each of his staff a new half-crown as a Christmas box. One of his employees was an odd-job man and regarded as rather simple. To him the employer held out the half-crown in one hand and a half-sovereign in the other. The old fellow grabbed the half-soverign and quickly putting it in his pocket said:

'Thank-ee sir, I took the little un as mother allus towd me not to be greedy.'
– S. Lummis, 32 High Street, Ipswich.

Drawing by Mary Tye

LOOKIN' ON

The late canon A.R. Upcher always enjoyed telling Suffolk stories as much as his hearers enjoyed listening. He used to tell the following story against himself. He was having his evening meal when the verger called. The verger sat talking to the cannon while he finished his meal and during the conversation the verger mentioned that his owd sow had recently pigged.

'Farrowed?' said the canon. 'Well done. How many has she?'

'Tharteen,' was the reply. 'But she hearn't got only twelve dills wass luck.'

'Oh dear,' replied the cannon. 'How does the poor little odd one get on?'

'Oh,' said the verger, 'that du the same as I'm a duin' – he sit and look on!– *J.C. Foulsham, Town House, Stradbroke, Diss.*

MAN FROM THE MINISTRY

In an Essex village a man from the ministry of something or other wanted to trace a certain Mr. Bramble who, he knew, lived in one of a group of almshouses. He was just about to turn in the communal gate when he met one of the almsmen coming out to draw water from the well on the village green. The conversation went like this:

Man from Ministry: 'Good morning. I wonder if you could tell me whether Mr. Bramble is in?'

Almsman (after putting down his bucket and reflecting for a moment):

'That he in't. He ha' just gorn out not a minute or two back.'

Man from Ministry: 'Dear me. That's a pity. I rather wanted to speak to him.'

Almsman: 'You did? Well you be a-speaking' to him now.'
– G.N. Gurney, Wagstaff Cottage, Dedham, Essex.

GIVE ME YOUR ANSWER DO

At the time when ladies began to wear bloomers for cycling, a party of young ladies was cycling along the Stoke Ferry Road on the way to Wereham. Meeting a real old Norfolkman on the roadside, one of the ladies asked:

'Is this the right way to Wereham?'

'Darned if Oi knows, Miss,' the old man replied. Oi never had no 'sperience with them things.'

– J.F.R. Buttle, Turret Cottage, Lynton, Devon.

NOTHING SERIOUS

I can still remember the answer given me by a Suffolk man at Hawkedon in 1920 when completing a life assurance proposal form. Receiving a negative reply to the question 'Is your father living?', I asked what was the cause of his death.

That true, honest face looked at me for a couple of moments and then he said:

'T'wern't nothing serious, bor.'

– Herbert S.H. Rolley, 4 Daily Street, Hamilton, New Zealand.

MISDIRECTION

Many years ago a dear old Methodist named Abram Claxton kept the Post Office at Wolferton and on one of his trips to London he wanted to visit the City Temple. He enquired the way and received the reply 'Do you want the Inns of Temple?'

No I doan't', said Abram. 'Yew mean Law, I mean Gorspel.'

– J.F.R. Buttle, Lynton, Devon.

THE QUIET WEEK

Old George's wife had died and he called in the undertaker who enquired when the funeral was to take place.

'I should like to bury the poor old gal tomorrow week, ' said George.

'Tommorow week! ' exclaimed the undertaker. 'That means a lapse of eight days. Have you any special reason for that?'

'Well it's like this, marster,' said George. 'We a-bin married now for 48 years and we allus vowed when we were a-courtin' that if we ever got married we'd hev a quiet week on our own. This is the only chance I ha' had so now I'm going to hevit.'

– G. Burroughs, Park View, Pin Mill, Nr. Ipswich.

CHANGE AT WICKHAM MARKET

One Tunstall lady to another:

'Did you hare my boy Bill a-bin called up?'

'Noo, Where be they a-sendin' of him?'

'Ong Kong, he say.'

Whereever's that?'

'Well, I don't rightly know but he tell me he hev ter change at Wickham Market.'

– Major R.C. Cole, 9 Victoria Avenue, Finchley, London, N.3.

THE BOMB AND THE EARWIG

During the first world war I went with some boys from my school to see a bomb crater in a neighbouring field. One boy ran ahead and when I looked down into the hole he held up his hand on which lay a small brown mess and said:

'Coo, sir I bet that gret owd bomb didn't half give that lettle owd earwig suthin.'

– E.L. Jenner, 8 New Row, Tanyard Lane, Steyning, Sussex.

IT'S ALL THE SAME

A lorry driver called at the village inn at Bramfield, near Halesworth, and asked the way to Dunwich. He was given detailed directions by one of the locals in the bar and departed. But no sooner had he gone than Harry said:

'Borb, you're tould him wrong. He'll git to Southwold thaat waay.'

'Thaat he oon't,' replied Bob.

'Thaat he will then, ' returned Harry and the two began to get rather heated. In the corner sat Winston, a retired sailor, who had so far remained silent, puffing at his pipe. But now he put an end to further argument by quietly remarking:

'Nivver moind. He'll git somewhere.'

– F.G.L. Crawshay, Helston, Greenway, Gerrard's Cross, Bucks.

A RARE SIGHT

At the meet at Bower House Farm, Polstead, I heard the following gem. The Sproughton Foot Beagles were in full cry past a cottage garden and a small boy was heard to shout to his mother:

'Hi, Mum! Hi, come on Mum! Run! There's a whole flock o' pups out here and a man a-blowin' a trumpit.'

– G.B. Webb, Stone Street, Boxford, Suffolk.

NOT TOO MUCH

A Victorian maid-of-all-work was going to a new 'place' and her mistress was giving her some good advice concluding with:

'And now, Mary, Mrs. Winterbottom is a very nice lady and you cannot do too much for her.'

Rising to the occasion Mary replied:

'I don't intend to, ma'am.'

– George Bloomfield, 47 Cliff Lane, Ipswich.

MARK OF RESPECT

In some Norfolk parishes it is usual, when the Bishop of the diocese visits, to hoist the flag on the church tower as a mark of respect.

One parish clerk hoisted the flag to half mast when a suffragan bishop came. Asked the reason, he promptly replied:

'Oh, ar, we put that roit up to the top when the Bishop come n' half mast when a sufferin' Bishop come.'

— John Durrant, Great Cornard, Suffolk.

DIAL '0'

Last year a farmer near ely asked one of his labourers to go to the telephone box and ring up the Potato Market. After about half an hour, the farmer went along to the box and found the man still inside. He asked if he had made the call and received the reply:

'Give a man a chance, Arfer, I bin lookin' through the T's for the last 'alf'our but, dammit, I can't find it nowheres.'

— P.J. Williams, Little Dowgate, Wisbech.

WELLWISHER

A family named Mason who lived at Leziate, Norfolk, had several children. One day the mother said to one of the older boys, named Stoutee:

'Look arter yar little brother while I'm out.'

Stoutee said:

'I wish little beggar wor dead.'

'Ah,' replied his mother. 'You are right there, Stoutee Bor.'

J.F.R. Buttle, Turret Cottage, Lynton, Devon.

SHARE AND SHARE ALIKE

When I was a lad in Norfolk, a friend and I went out bird catching. After we had caught some sparrows and larks we agreed to divide them up so I counted out:

'A lark for me and a sparrow for you. A sparrow for you and a lark for me' until we had shared them.

'Count 'em again', said my friend. 'I've got all sparrows.'

So I counted them all out again—'A sparrow for you and a lark for me. A lark for me and a sparrow for you. . .'

'Yes, that's fair enough,' he said when I'd finished. 'But somehow I've still got all sparrows.'

P.P.H. Bailey, 40 Stroud Road, Shirley, Solihull, Warwickshire.

A LOVELY WEDDING

When I recently visited a woman in a Suffolk village I was given a description of a wedding the family had attended the week before. On enquiring what the bride wore for the occasion I was informed that she 'looked wholly nice. she wore an off-grey costume and pink necessities.'

– *Mrs. Kathleen M. Brunger, Valley Cottage, Horham, Nr. Diss.*

DELAYING TACTICS

A Norfolk grave-digger of over 80 was digging a grave when the vicar came along for a chat. He asked the old man how deep he dug the graves and received the following reply:

'Them I don't like I put down another two feet so's they'll be late for the resurrection.'

– *F.E. Radway, Church Green, Ramsey, Huntingdon.*

Drawing by Paul Hogarth

THE DOCTOR KNOWS BEST

Two brothers, both bachelors, used to live near Woolpit. Their surname was Theobald, locally pronounced 'Tebbled'.

One of them was very ill and near his end and when the doctor called he said'

'Ah, poor fellow, he's gone.'

But a weak voice from the bed announced:

'I een't dead, doctor.'

Whereupon his brother said:

'Howd yar tongue. The doctor know better'n yow.'

– *R. Chaplin, 121 Valley Road, Ipswich.*

THE WATER-SPLASH

A motorist, coming to a water-splash across the road, asked a local countryman who was standing on the footbridge:

'Can I get through?'

'Yes,' said the local man.

The motorist got half way through when the car stopped, its wheels and engine pretty well covered by the water. Shouted the angry motorist:

'I thought you said I could get through?'

'Well I jest see some ducks go across so I thought you could.'

– *W.G. Munnings, The Rookery, Weybread, Diss.*

Alarmed and angry gentleman having been narrowly missed by speeding 'learner': 'You'll never pass your test!' Equally alarmed 'learner': 'Dew I dew, yew on't live to see it.'

SIMPLE ARITHMETIC

Having spent a quarter of a century as headmaster of Helmingham School, my father has a host of anecdotes of school life. My favourite concerns an arithmetic class in which a rather backward pupil was being questioned in fractions.

'Now boy'. said my father, 'which would you prefer—a third of a cske or a fifth of a cake?'

Without hesitation came the reply: 'A fifth of a cake, sir!'

Father was naturally very cross and demanded to know the reason for such an answer and the reply was again rapidly forthcoming:

'Please, sir, I 'in't all that fond o' cake.'

– *S.H. Thompson, Barle Corner, Dulverton, Somerset.*

THE SIXPENNY SIDE

Fifty or sixty years ago in this village there was a farmer who was a good sort and would help anyone. Unfortunately he was almost stone deaf.

There was also a man who used to do cattle droving and who was usually hard up. One day he met the old farmer and shouted at him:

'Lend me sixpence, Mr. M.'

The farmer put his hand up to his other ear and said:

'What did you say?'

Going round to the other side the drover shouted:

'Lend me half a crown, Mr. M.'

The farmer shook his head. 'You've got the wrong ear,' he said. 'Go you round to the tanner side.'

– *R.E. Jolley, Lidgate, Newmarket, Suffolk.*

FIRST ONE TODAY

A man was hunting with Norwich Stag Hounds and had a bad fall. By the time he had sorted himself out and caught his horse the hounds had gone. After a time he saw an old roadman and said:

'Have you seen the hounds?'

The roadman replied: 'You're the fust one I ha' sin today.'

– G.B. Webb, Stone Street, Boxford, Suffolk.

GIANT HALES OF SOMERTON

A brother of giant hales of Somerton told my father that he was in Gt. Yarmouth market place one day and picked up a tooth-comb which broke in his hand. Immediately, the owner of the stall, a woman, said:

'That's a penny.'

Hales paid the penny and then told the woman what sort of a person she was and what kind of goods she sold. Then he added to my father:

'O' course, if I han't paid my penna I couldn't a-said nothen.'

– Wm. Pratt, 43 Lansdowne Avenue, Slough, Bucks.

HOW TO CURE A COLD

A tradesman went into the village inn, said he had a bad cold and asked if anyone could tell him how to get rid of it.

'Yes,' said one of the customers. 'Jest you do as I tell you.' Everyone listened with interest. 'Dew yew buy a bottle o' rum, bor, take that hoom and drink half of it. Then go to bed and git yar missus to bring the other half upstairs to you. Then dew yew drink the remainder and think of all the people yew ha' robbed and if that don't sweat the cold out o' yew northen will.'

– A. Parnell, Bear's Grove, Salhouse, Norwich.

MR. BUGG OF LODDON

When I saw that picture of Loddon in a recent issue my mind flashed back to a conversation that took place on the telephone way back in the 20's. It occurred in a grocer's shop in Loddon the name of whose proprietor was Mr. Bugg.

A telephone subscriber in Norwich had asked for a Loddon number. For some unexplained reason he was connected with Mr. Bugg's grocer's shop and the phone was answered by the assistant who had a broad Norfolk dialect.

'Hallo,' he said.

Subscriber in Norwich: 'Is that Loddon?'

Assistant: 'Bugg o' Loddon.'

Subscriber in Norwich: 'B———you, too!' And he hung up the receiver.

– Herbert S.H. Rolley, 2 R.D. Ohaupo, New Zealand.

NO NEED FOR A DEVIL

My father used to tell of an old farm labourer who worked for a very hard master at Clavering, Essex. The master was not only a slave-driver but was harsh towards his wife and family. One day, after an unusually violent outburst from him, the labourer remarked with much feeling:

'Our master is a real bad man. Ef the devil doon't hev he, what's the goodd t' hev a devil?'

– Irene Cranwell, Faerie Cottage, Chrishall, Nr. Royston, Herts.

ADAM AND EVE

The infants were hearing the story of Adam and Eve. Asked afterwards:

'How did God punish them for being so disobedient?' a small boy replied: 'He put the stick acorst 'em.'

– M.A. Checkland, The Old Rectory, Felthorpe, Norwich.

Drawing by Mary Tye

INVALID'S DIET

An old man who lived at Walton, Felixstowe, had spent quite a portion of his life in prison for chicken stealing. On one of these occasions a warder brought him his breakfast of bread and water. The old man looked at it and said:

'I ain't ill, sir. I can eat eggs and bacon.'

—Wm. Dent, 7 Copleston Road, Ipswich.

NOT LIKELY

When the new churchyard was made at Cavendish some years ago. Walter and old George were leaning over the gate, wholly disapproving.

'Well, bor,' said George, 'when Oi doi, if Oi'm alive and well, I oon't lie theere.'

—Miss Dorothy Williams, The Street, Sturmer, Nr. Haverhill, Suffolk.

GOOD FOR SALES

An East Anglian yokel, gazing at a mug at the top of which the froth had subsided, said to the landlord:

'You know, John, you'd sell a lot more beer if you filled the mugs up.'

—R.H. Futter, Thwaite St. Mary, Nr. Bungay, Suffolk.

THE BOGUS TELEGRAM

Joe and Harry were like peas in a pod. The only subject on which they differed was football. Joe supported the Arsenal while Harry's life-long idols were Aston Villa.

In the early 20's, before the advent of radio, Joe made (for him) the rare visit to Highbury to see the Gunners play the Villa, promising to send a wire to Harry after the match, thus avoiding the wait for the Sunday papers.

The much-looked-forward-to telegram duly arrived in the village and was copied out by the local post-mistress and despatched by a passer-by to Harry. Surrounded by interested friends Harry opened the telegram and read aloud:

'Arsenal 4, Villa 0.'

A look of contempt came over his face. Slowly he tore up the envelope and its contents and said to the assembled group:

'You can't fool me wi' that stuff. Thut ain't owd Joe's writin!'

— Kenneth B. Ward, 97 Head Street, Halstead.

SYLVESTER AND THE PARSON

In Flempton about 60 years ago when I was a child there lived a surly old man named Sylvester Holmes. He was a roadman. One day the Rev. Holden called out the time of day to him and as he made no reply the reverend gentleman stopped his pony trap and asked Sylvester the reason. Sylvester just gave a grunt.

'Surely you know who I am,' said the clergyman. 'I am the Rev. John Holden, Rector of Lackford and Lord of the Manor.'

At this Sylvester looked up and said: 'Well, you a-got a damn good job. Just you mind and keep it.'

— Mrs. B.E. Keen, Flempton, Suffolk.

IN PRAISE OF BEER

I remember a man in my village who was nicknamed 'Shimmy', a corruption of chemise. His brothers, incidentally, were 'Shut' (shirt) and 'Britches' (breeches). Shimmy was fond of his pint of beer and the vicar was reproving him one day, saying that the money he spent on drink would buy a nice joint of meat. But Shimmy, who stuttered, said:

'B-b-but beer heen't got no boons in, sir.'

Another character was Billy, the butcher's man, to whom my mother used to give a pint of my father's brew which had a reputation for strength. My mother, who did not like beer, said:

'I can't think how you can get the stuff down, Billy.'

'Tha's easy, Mam,' he replied. 'Yow jest howd yar hid back, oopen yar showders and that'll run down all right.'

– *R. Chaplin, 121 Valley Road, Ipswich.*

CLERK TO THE HINS

An Essex farmer had bought an incubator of a rather early make. He explained to his old farm-worker who looked after the poultry:

'I want you to put an 'O' on one side of the eggs and an 'X' on the other side and turn the eggs every day.'

Old Thomas said to his master: 'Oi've worked for yew, man and boy, these larst 50 years but Oi'll be danged if Oi'll be clerk to these here hins.'

– *R.E. Everard, Wendycot, Green Lane, Walton-on-the-Naze, Essex.*

OUR VILLAGE

A Suffolk school mistress asked her pupils to write an essay on the amenities of the village.

One wrote: 'This is a large village. We have two doctors and one cemetery.'

– *The Rev. R.S. Crompton, 30 Stone Street, Boxford, Colchester.*

Drawing by Nancy Blyth

THE BISHOP AND THE BOY

A lady who employed a houseboy had invited the bishop to stay with her. The boy was told to say, when he knocked on the bedroom door in the morning: 'Here is the boy with your hot water, my Lord.'

So as to make sure that he wouldn't forget, the boy practised saying the words over and over again and when the time came said:

'Here is the Lord with your hot water my boy.'

– *John G. Golden, Church Street, North Repps, Cromer.*

ROPEY BEER

Many years ago, Sam Wright of East Bergholt was working on a farm where the farmer used to brew his own beer. One day the farmer brought him some and asked how it tasted.

'Just right,' said Sam.

'How do you mean, "Just right"?'

'Well,' said Sam, 'if it had been any better I wouldn't have got it and if it had been any wusser I couldn't have drunk it.'

– *Jim Cole, Box 17, Kellerberrin, West Australia.*

RECORD CATCH

A Norfolk angler had caught nothing all day. Returning home in the evening with empty frail and not wishing to meet anybody he avoided the road. Climbing the bank of the river he saw what appeared to him to be a man with arms outstretched describing a catch. He shouted at the top of his voice:

'It's a blan and ruddy lie.'

Imagine his chagrin when, on getting nearer, he discovered it was a scarecrow.

– *J. Williams, 21 Belle Vue Road, Cinderford, Glos.*

OUTPUT

An old man and a younger one were muck spreading on a farm one day when the farmer, who had been watching them from the gate, walked up to them and said to the younger one:

'George, I've been watching you two at work and I've noticed that the old man is spreading two forkfuls to your one.'

'Yes, master, I know', said George. 'I keep telling the silly old fule about it but he takes no notice of me.'

– *Cyril D. Bruce, Beacon Hill, Stone Lodge Lane, Ipswich.*

LATE MORNINGS

Some old friends of ours who usually retire quite early were having a few late nights due to the christmas festivities. One of them glanced at the clock and said:

'It's time we were home. It was morning before we went to bed last night and it'll soon be morning again tonight.'

— Miss. E. Carter, Bury Road, Denston, Newmarket.

HOW TO GIT DOWN

During 'Haysel' Bill, working on top of the stack, wanted to come down and discovered that someone had removed the ladder.

'Oi can't git down,' he called out to his mate below.

'Jest yow shut ya oies an' walk abowt an' yew'll git down quick enough' he replied.

— L. Sewell, Hall Street, Long Melford.

GROUNDS FOR COMPLAINT

William was a farm worker who had a habit of thinking aloud. One morning on his way to work he was overheard expressing a grievance against his wife.

'No, Betty, mor,' he said, 'it ain't fair. You allust gie me the fust cup o' tea and the larst cup o' coffee.'

— Miss. K. Ford, 5 Golden Dog Lane, Norwich.

MUTUAL SILENCE

A labourer had gone to a new job and after a few weeks was asked how he was getting along with his new master.

'Well,' he replied, 'he en't said nothen to me.' Then after a pause: And come to that I en't said nothen to him.'

— F.J. Woods, 'Woodside', Morton on the Hill, Norwich.

THE MAN WHO MARRIED MABEL

My great aunt, the late Mrs. Keeble, who many will remember, owned a pork butcher's shop at the junction of Duke Street and Fore Hamlet, Ipswich. She was well-known for her straight dealing and candid comment.

For many years a local farmer supplied her with eggs for resale. They were delivered by the farmer's daughter, a timid and simple soul who seemed incapable of saying anything other than 'I've brought the eggs, Mrs. Keeble' and 'Good morning'.

This ritual continued year in and year out until one day a dapper little man dressed in check coat, breeches and buskins appeared carrying the familiar basket and also saying: 'I've brought the eggs, Mrs. Keeble.'

'What's wrong with Mabel?' asked my great aunt.

The little man looked uncomfortable and said: 'Well , as a matter of fact she's getting married.'

'Married!' ejaculated Mrs. Keeble. 'Whoever is fool enough to marry her?'

The man dropped his eyes and said: 'Well, to tell you the truth, I am.'

— Mrs. F.R. Wright, 13 Waverley Road, Eaton, Norwich.

OBSTACLE

This story is told by Kathleen Long, the famous pianist, who was born near Bury St. Edmunds.

My father had one of the first motor cars ever to be seen in West Suffolk. He was driving after dark down a long and twisting hill. As he approached the bottom he came to a hump-backed bridge at a sharp corner and suddenly saw a herd of cows scattered all over the road. No one was with them.

He hooted furiously for some minutes, quite in vain, his temper rising with every hoot. At last a door a couple of hundred yards up the road opened slowly and a slit of light appeared.

Very, very slowly, down the road stumped an old drover, his cap on top of a large forelock and an old red check scarf round his neck. He held a large nobbly stick in his hand, with which he hit the road.

When he came within hailing distance my father let fly:

'How dare you leave those cows unattended on this bad corner. What the so and so do you mean by it? I might have had a fearful accident, you old fool.'

The old boy gazed at my father with cool curiosity and let him rage on for several minutes. At last, when he had exhausted his invection, the old drover said, very quietly, very slowly:

'Sharl I tell you suthin'?'

'Well, what is it?' said my father impatiently.

'They h'aint cowses. They're bullocks.'

– J. Course, 3 London Road, Royston.

PARDON

Many years ago we had a dear old parson–his name was Wayman–who had become slightly deaf. One day, just as my sister and I were off cycling, he came along on his bicycle. He got off to have a word with us and after a bit my sister said:

'How is Mrs. Wayman today?'

'Very nice', he said, 'but rather windy.'

– Miss. W.S. Dawson, 30 Swan Street, Boxford.

I've helped yew a bit, I've laced yer boots up ready.

A LITTLE HELP

Old George had living with him on the farm a young man who was always late in getting up in the morning. So one morning George called:

'Bill, you be late agin this mornin'. I've helped yew a bit. I've laced yer boots up ready for yer.'

– *E.W. Jennings, Avalon, Alresford, Colchester, Essex.*

HIGH STREET

While on holiday at Lowestoft I happened to ask a local if I was in the High Street.

'Ah, yes,' he said, 'but that int high down the bott'm, thass low.'

– *R.D. Peartree, 43 Hilborough, Thetford.*

SUPPLY AND DEMAND

I used to live in Loddon, Norfolk, and one day called at the local trefoil and grist mill, which was powered by electricity. It was a windy day and one of the millers asked me:

'Don't yew know why there is s' much wind these days? Tha's cause there int the windmills t'use it up.'

–*J.S. Hacon, Cumberland House, Mistley, Manningtree, Essex.*

WHY HE SOLD THE SOW

A man was telling a friend about the sow he used to own.

'But I got rid o'her,' he said. 'She worn't n' good. The first time she pigged she didn't hev any and the next time she hed only tew and they eat each other.'

– *A. Parnell, Salhouse, Norwich.*

CHRISTMAS GIFT

A battered 'vintage' car clanked on to Foundry bridge, Norwich, was held up by the lights and stalled. The driver climbed out and started cranking to get it started again.

Immediately behind him was a brand new black and silver Cadillac. The harder he cranked, the louder the Cadillac hooted at him.

Finally, red of face and short of wind, he turned to the Cadillac's owner and said quietly:

'And what else did y'have for Christmas?'

– W. Chilvers, 131 Cecil Rd., Norwich.

EXPLANATION

The Parson took for the text of his sermon, 'Who are these arrayed in white and whence came they?'

Up leapt Old Giles at the back of the church:

'My two nieces from London.'

–A.J. Sargent, 459 S. McDonnell Ave, Los Angeles 22.

UNCORROBORATED EVIDENCE

A Suffolk girl, aged 13, was asked by her Sunday-school teacher:

'King Pharoah's daughter found the little boy Moses in the bullrushes, didn't she?'

'She said so, miss.'

–From 'Memories of a School Inspector' by A.J. Swinburne.

UNIVERSAL PROVIDER

Some years ago, a landgirl entered a small general store in Filby and asked the man behind the counter if he sold powder.

'Certainly Miss', said the man. 'Do you want face, emery, gun or flea powder?'

– C. Newman, Constitutional Club, Northumberland Avenue, London

FISH SUPPER

When putting the cat out for the night my grandfather always used to encourage it by shouting:

'Out ya git, ya lazy owd thing. Thas herrin' fallen out a' the moon.'

– R.G. Gladwell, 14 Victoria Road, Oulton Broad.

JUST IN TIME

In a Norfolk village a couple had been courting for some years and suddenly made up their minds to get married.

On the Sunday when the banns were just about to be read the bridegroom-to-be rushed into church shouting:

'Hi, hi, hi! Shush, shush! I ha' changed my mind.'

– Mrs. Blanche Keen, 394 Ham Green, Holt, near Trowbridge, Wilts.

BREAKING THE JOURNEY

During the sixties there was considerable emigration to America and one mid-Suffolk worthy thought he would venture. Talking to him in the local, a neighbour remarked that it must be a long way to go.

'Well,' said John, 'we count on sleepin' at Debenham the first night so that'll kinda break the journey.'

– G. Bloomfield, Cliff Lane, Ipswich.

THEM RABBITS, THE VARMINTS

Two farmers met at the local market and the following conversation took place:

'Wal, John, bor, how now?'

'Oi don't know. Tom, Oi fare in a mess. There be that many owd rabbits round moi way Oi reckon Oi shall hetta sell out. Blarst, moi wheat int half a crop.'

'Don't yew do nawthen o' the sort, John. Dew yew go with the toimes– lay yar filds down a grass an' keep cows.'

John turned this idea over in his mind and eventually decided to take his friend's advice. As the months went by, however, he found that the rabbits ate off the grass just as badly as they had eaten his corn. Later he met Tom again.

'Oi reckon you made a fule out o' me, Tom,' he said. 'Oi put down a tidy bit o' grass but, blarst, they owd rabbits ha' got that down that short they are loike to starve, let alone moi owd cows.'

Tom scratched his head and produced another idea.

'Dew you ketch they owd rabbits, John, bor, an' tarn thim into potted meat,' he said.

John swore roundly at his friend but in a last despairing venture set to work and soon had established a fine reputation for his potted meat. But all good things must come to an end sooner or later and the last conversation on the subject one market day went like this:

'How now, Tom, bor?'

'Oh, kinder middlin', loike. What are yew a-doin' of?'

'What dew yew mean, bor?'

'Wal, yar owd potted meat. I proper took ta that at one toime but that int what that used to be. What are yew a-doin' of?'

'Wal, Tom, bor, we're gittin' short o' rabbits so whin Skinner, the hoss slaughterer, hev a young hoss doi he let me hev a bit o' meat ta mix wi' the rabbit.'

'How much hoss dew yew put in, John, bor, cos that be wa's a-maken all the difference tew yar potted meat.'

'Wa, fifty-fifty, Tom, bor–one hoss, one rabbit.'

– A.E. Orford, 7 St Mary's Cresent, Walton, Felixstowe.

INVOCATION

An old boy who lives down our lane was rather dubious about his seed potatoes, as they were of poor quality. I happened to pass when he was covering them in after planting and I overheard him talking to himself. He said:

'Dew yew doon't come up, up yew come.'

— *Edward E. Taylor, The Cottage, Lawn Lane, Downham, Isle of Ely.*

LEGITIMATE COMMENT

I used to farm at Capel St. Mary. One day I was wheeling my young son out in his pram and, meeting an old employee, we stopped to have a chat. He peered into the pram and presently said:

'Ha, marster, yar missus niver wint far astray arter he,' and stumped off.

— *P.O. Packard, P.O. Box 31, Malkerns, Swaziland.*

BREEDING

A Mr. William Brown, a big gent in his own estimation, made some proposals at a parish meeting which were objected to by a farmer. Highly enraged, he said to the farmer:

'Sir, do you know that I have been to two universities?'

'Well, sir, what of that?' said the farmer. 'I had a calf that sucked two cows and the observation I made was, the more he sucked, the greater calf he grew.'

— *Miss. Lily Palmer, 88 Clay Street, Soham, Ely, Cambs.*

MARKSMANSHIP

I joined the Old 4th Suffolk Volunteers in 1903. The first time we went to Sizewell butts for shooting practice we fired seven shots each at 200 yards range. One recruit missed the target with every shot.

The Sergeant Instructor said to him:

'Put a bullet in the breech, go to the back of the butts and see if you can shoot yourself.'

The recruit went off obediently and after a while we heard a shot. Then, to our surprise, he reappeared and said:

'Sorry, Sergeant, Missed again.'

— *E.H. Kerrison, 36 Hellards Road, Stevenage, Herts.*

BACKWARD

Going to work early one morning, an old Suffolk farmhand stopped to light his pipe. Because of the wind he turned round and lit the match under his jacket.

A few minutes later he met one of his mates, who said:

'Why are you going home, Ben?'

'Cor blast,' said Ben. 'I never turned round after lighting me pipe.'

— *Mrs. A.R. Chinery, Juana, Acton, Sudbury.*

TIED DOWN

Our buses carry parcels from one place to another for a small charge. We were waiting at a bus stop one day, when a girl came hurrying up, handed a letter to the conductor and asked him to deliver it at an address in the next village.

'Sorry, miss. No letters. Only parcels.'

The girl looked crest-fallen and said it was urgent. Our bus conductors are mostly kind-hearted fellows.

'Tell you what,' he counselled. 'Take it in to Bert here' (the tobacconist). 'Ask him to put a bit of string round it and it'll go as a parcel.' Which she did, and which proves that the East Anglian is not only a humorist but a man of resource.

— *Margaret Nicholson, Meadow Way, Ufford, Woodbridge.*

Drawing by R. Sell

MILK TRAY

An old lady had just engaged a new maid. One of the duties was to take a glass of hot milk into the drawing room at night. The girl carried the tumbler in her hand but the old lady told her:

'I like my milk on a tray.'

So the next evening the girl poured the milk into a tray and as she handed it to her mistress enquired:

'Will yar lap it or will yar hev a spune?'

– Mrs. K. Chapman, 14 Nightingale Place, Orford, Woodbridge.

THE COST OF SALVATION

It happened to be a very gallant rescue by Old So-and-so of a summer visitor who had been foolhardy enough, in the face of all warnings, to venture out to sea by himself, sailing a 12-foot dinghy.

A terrific squall came up and he caught it. Snatched from the very jaws of death, the visitor, when landed, presented his rescuer with–one shilling. Relating the story afterwards the old man said:

'An' what d'ye think he give me? One shillun'. Said he couldn't afford no more! "Yew duzzy fool," I say, "what did yew goo an' be drowned for if ye couldn't afford to be saved" '

– Miss. Grace Pickthall, 76 Canon Street, Winchester, Hants.

YOU CAN'T MISS IT

A motorist stopped a Suffolk farm boy and enquired for a certain place. The boy replied:

'Dew yaow goo as far as Wiggs' farm, then tarn agin tew haystacks, then howd to the laft past the parson's, down a hill, over the bridge, then take the second road to the right and if yew keep a-goin' right yaow can't goo wrong.'

– R.E. Everard, Wendycot, Green Lane, Walton-on-the-Naze, Essex.

SOME HOLE

When Harry, a grown boy, paid his first visit to the seaside, he stood on the cliff tip and garped. Then he said to his pal:

'Cor, cor! What a grut owd hole! And what a lot o' water in't.'

– Mrs. R. Clover, Buxhall Mills, Stowmarket.

BETTER THAN NOTHING

My late father, the Rev. C. Deane, when Vicar of Happisburgh with Walcot, visited a parishioner to commiserate with her on the loss of her husband and she replied:

'Ah well, he was company but he worn't no comfort!'

– Miss. W.M. Deane, Castle Acre, King's Lynn, Norfolk.

I wonder how much she'd charge to pluck an owd hin!
– Based on a story sent in by F. Thrower, 14 Ransome Road, Scole, Diss.

A BIT OF ENCOURAGEMENT FIRST

A farmer asked his friend to a day's shooting. At the first drive he shot a partridge and it fell into a ditch. The farmer's dog went after it and as he didn't come out he went across to look and saw the partridge's legs disappearing down the dog's throat.

'Hi!' he shouted, 'Your b––––– dog has eaten my partridge.'

'You don't want to worry about that a mite,' was the reply. 'He on't work till he's eaten three.'
– G.B. Webb, Boxford, Suffolk.

NO LOSS OF CUSTOM

The parson was one day taking a stroll through his Norfolk village when he happened to meet old Tom and with a 'Very good morning!' he remarked:

'Tom, I haven't seen you for a long time. You used to come to church so regularly and I've been rather worried by your absence.'

'Well, you needn't worra, sar,' said Tom. 'Yow hin't lorst my custom. I don't go anywhere ilse.'
– R.M. Neale, 62 Giffords Cross Road, Corringham, Essex.

IRREPRESSIBLE

Many years ago Mr. Pettiward the Squire of Finborough, used to ride on horseback round the countryside. Wanting to find out who owned a nice looking lot of pigs, he addressed a man leaning over the fence looking at them:

'Morning, George. Who do those pigs belong to?'

GEORGE, pointing:

'Whoy, that grit owd sow there.'

SQUIRE: 'No no, I mean who's the master?'

GEORGE', again pointing:

'That little owd b——— there. 'E can whip the lot on 'em.

The squire rode on and, meeting the head stockman later, said:

'George was trying to be funny this morning. Just take it out of him, will you?'

HEAD STOCKMAN, later to George:

'Squire's just been a-talking to me 'bout yew. He says he wants to give yew a job up at the Hall.'

GEORGE: 'Oh? What's that?'

STOCKMAN: 'He wants yew to goo up there and play the fool.'

GEORGE: 'What? Is 'e goin' to give you the sack or is e' goin' to keep two on us?'—

Dr. H.S. Gaskell, 17 Recreation Road, Stowmarket.

PIG FOOD

I remember overhearing the following conversation many years ago at Stoke Ferry station:

'What are you giving your pigs, now, Jim?'

'I mostly gives 'em a bit of straw.'

'Ah! But when it's a bad year for straw and there ain't much straw about?'

'Ah! Bless me,' said Jim. 'When it's a bad year for straw and there ain't much straw about, well—there you be.'

—Canon O. G. Bolton, Ely Cathedral.

CO-OPERATION

A relief organist for Easter evening thought it advisable to cycle to the church to ascertain the form of service. When he arrived, the first person he encountered was the organ blower. After some preliminary enquiries, the old blower blurted out:

'I suppose you'll end the service with the Hallelujah Chorus?' To which the organist replied in the negative, as he had not got the necessary music. Heatedly the old blower said:

'We've had it played at the end of Easter Day for the past 40 years. You can play what you like. I shall pump the Hallelujah Chorus.

—Stanley Last, Appletree Cottage, Dedham, Essex.

CHURCH BELLS

A band of young bell ringers at practice were being helped by an experienced man. Suddenly one let go of the rope and his teacher said:

'Mind what yew dew with that rope, bor. Don't hang me or you'll ha' ter keep my missus.'

A.I.H., Helmingham Road, Otley, near Ipswich.

NO RELATION

As I entered an Inn at Wells, Norfolk, I saw George standing at the corner of the bar looking most unhappy.

He told me he had just received a telegram stating that his father, to whom he was very attached, had died suddenly.

I saw him in the inn the following day but this time exultant.

'What has made you so happy?', I said.

'I've just found out that that telegram should have been delivered to my brother and not me' was the reply.

—E.A.R. Hampton, 1 Weston Park, London, N.8.

GREAT NEED

There was a small, noncomformist sect who had a fund for brothers in distress. One night a man whose house had been burnt down was summoned before the chief elders.

'How much do you need?' one of them asked him.

The man, unwilling to commit himself and eyeing the pile of money on the table, replied:

'Brother, I need it all.'

Angela Thornton, (aged 12), 2 Hazel Close, Leigh-on-Sea, Essex.

THE DANGERS OF MATRIMONY

Mary kept house for John, an elderly farmer, and for a long time had endeavoured to persuade him to marry her. One evening they were seated on either side of the fire and in the middle were two cats curled up together, sleeping soundly.

'Look at they cats,' said Mary. 'They look nice and comfortable. Why can't we git married and live together like they?'

'Ah,' replied John, 'but dew yew tie they up togither and see how they foight.'

—Wm. Dent, 7 Copleston Road, Ipswich.

Drawing by R. Sell

GOOD PAY

One night my brother was coming home on his motor-bike just as the men were turning out of the'Lion'. An old man was in the road and Fred's front wheel went between his legs and knocked him over backwards. Fred asked:

'Are you hurt, Sam?'

'Oh, my belly!' said Sam.

'Here's half a crown for you, Sam.'

Replied Sam: 'You can do it again for that.'

W.G. Munnings, The Rookery Nook, Weybread, Diss.

'Mum, it's Mrs. Jackson. She wants a double whisky on the quiet.'

Contributed by T. Thompson, Walberswick, drawing by Jennifer Kent

YOU HAVE BEEN WARNED

I was camping in a field close to Overstrand. The next field happened to be where the farmer kept his fowls. One morning he was in a very bad mood and, when he came to collect the eggs one of the cocks began to crow lustily.

'Shut up, yer b—— fowl,' he shouted twice.

The cock still crowed, then:

'If yer don't, I'll ring yer b—— neck,'

Still the cock crowed. Without any more ado the farmer snatched it up, wrung its neck, threw it down and said:

'There. Perhaps that'll larn yer to do as yer told next time.'

—B.R. Tuck, Galanthus, Hr: Bojewyan, Pendeen, Cornwall.

ENCORE

About 50 years ago I spent some weeks staying at the one and only inn of a small Norfolk village, mine host of which was also the organist of the little church.

Harvest Festival was fixed for early afternoon one Sunday which turned out very hot and mine host had a number of customers at lunch time. So well did they partake of good cheer that the organist fell asleep during the sermon and snored loudly. On being given a prod by one of the choirmen, the congregation was somewhat put out when they heard him exclaim loudly:

'Orl ri'. Fill 'em up again!'

—J.B.L. Tolhurst, The Chantry, Walsingham.

HADDISCOE EXPRESS

The train from Manchester arrived late at Norwich and left me only a few seconds in which to catch my connection to Haddiscoe.

There was no railway official on the platform except the guard, who was waving off the train, and there seemed to be only one passenger. I put my question to him:

'Does this train go through Haddiscoe, please?'

'Ah, bor!' he replied.

Ten minutes later my companion looked across at me and completed his sentence.

'Ah, bor,' he said, 'it goes through Haddiscoe but I don't know that it stop there.'

—W.R.C. Chapman, Headmaster, Firth Park Grammar School. The Brushes, Barnsley Road, Sheffield, 5.

SENSIBLE TO THE LAST

The old farmer was dying and his wife and a few neighbours were sitting by his bed. After a long silence the old man whispered:

'I owe Farmer Brown five pounds.'

His wife commented: 'There he go—ramblin' again.'

After another long silence he again started to whisper, this time saying that Farmer Harvey owed him 10 pounds.

At this his wife cried triumphantly:

'There he go again—sensible to the last.'

—Mrs. E.C. Lusted, Burwash Common, Elchingham, Sussex.

MAKING DO

During the first world war Suffolk farmers were often so short of men that pig sties and hen houses did not get their customary cleaning out. The quarterly 'clean out' was left for months longer. So neglected were the hen houses at one particular farm that the muck had almost reached the perches.

Noticing this when walking round the farm, a visitor expressed his suprise and asked the inefficient farmer what he was going to do about it. The only reply he got was:

'Oh, don't worry, old man. I'll lift the perches.'

—Walter Tye, 675 Foxhall Road,Ipswich.

THE EXPERT

A farmer was taking a few friends round his farm and they showed an interest in an apple tree bearing some nice-looking fruit. They asked its name and the farmer called to an old man working nearby:

'Come here, George. You've been about here a lot longer than I have. Can you tell us what apple this is?'

The old man dropped his hoe, came over, looked at the tree and said: 'I think 'haps I can tell yer if yer'll gimme one to try.'

He was given one and after taking a good bite and chewing it for a minute or more, said: 'Ah! I thought I knowed! Why, tha's a airten apple that is.'

—F.W. Myhill, Hethel Red House, Braconash, Norwich.

REWARD FOR VIGILANCE

Years ago, around Christmas time, with rough weather causing unemployment, there was always a certain amount of chicken stealing from the allotments bordering the town.

A local policeman, who had a very high opinion of himself, heard that a certain hen-run was to be raided the next night. Armed with a can of hot tea and a spare overcoat he hid himself in a clump of bushes prepared to catch the thieves red-handed. Perished with cold, he stayed until dawn.

But nothing happened. On his way home to breakfast he called at his own allotment to feed his chickens.

They were all gone.

—Herbert Ives, Vancouver House, Vancouver Avenue, King's Lynn.

IT MIGHT A-BIN WORSE

Mrs. Hawkins was a confirmed optimist. No matter what calamity befell her or the community her comment was always: 'Well, it might a-bin wuss!'

Her husband, who was a bricklayer, was putting the finishing courses on a tall chimney when the entire top gave way, precipitating him to the ground with fatal results.

When a neighbour broke the sad news to her Mrs. Hawkins commented as usual:

'Well, it might a-bin wuss!'

The neighbour, shocked, said: 'You've lost your poor, dear husband. How could it be worse?'

'Well,' said Mrs. Hawkins, 'if he'd a-fell on another man and killed him—that would a-bin wuss!'

—Ernest A. Hutchinson, 1710 Bushnell Avenue, Sth. Pasadena, California, U.S.A.

POSTSCRIPT

A widow was telling a crony that she had ordered an elaborate grave-stone for her dear departed husband who had every week given her his pay packet unopened.

'Ah,' said her friend, 'but did you know he worked two evenings a week for Farmer Brown?'

The widow was furious and went straight to the stone-mason, asking him to delete the letters 'R.I.P.' The stonemason said it wasn't possible to make the alteration.

'Well, can you add a line?' the widow asked and when the mason agreed there was room:

'Right!' said the widow, 'After "R.I.P." put "Till I come"!'

—Miss B.D. Barker, Post Office, North Pickenham, Swaffham.

Drawing by Nancy Blyth

NEVER TWO DAYS ALIKE

Two women, each going to the seaside for the day, had become acquainted in the train.

'Thass a rummun that hatter pour wi' rain t'day, en't it? Now yisterday was a lovely day, weren't it?'

'Yis and so was the day afore.'

'Thass what I say—we niver git two days alike, do we?'

'No, that we don't.'

—Miss H.Feaviour, Harleston, Norfolk.

TEW, FOWER, SIX, EIGHT

Owd Sam was a shepherd. Indeed he was a good shepherd. He tended a flock of 200. Unfortunately, he couldn't read or write. His master knew this and suspected he could not count, either, and he wondered how the old man would know if any sheep were missing.

One day the master decided to put Owd Sam to the test. As the sheep were about to pass through a narrow way allowing just sufficient room for two to walk abreast the farmer said:

'Sam, just count them as they go through"

The old chap pointed a finger and commenced, in true Suffolk dialect:

'Tew, fower, six, aight, half a score, there go tew more, there's another tew, tew more, there go another tew . . .' until all the flock had passed through. Then, turning to the farmer: 'Just as I thowt. All there. 'Xactly tew hundred.'

—S. Lummis, 32 High Street, Ipswich.

A-JAWIN' AND A-JAWIN'

Two old Norfolkmen met almost daily to sit by the roadside quite content to remain silent for long periods. One day Bill broke the silence to ask:

'How's yar wife a-gittin' on now, Chaarlie?'

'Well,' was the reply, 'I don't rightly know wass the matter with har. She keep on a-jawin' and a-jawin'.'

A prolonged silence. Then:

'Thass a rum un about yar wife, Chaarlie. What du she keep a-jawin' about?'

'I dunno. She doon't saay.'

—Mrs. Elsie Lingwood, Bosmere House, Martlesham, Woodbridge.

WHAT A SON-IN-LAW

During the 1914-18 war a good many overseas troops contacted relatives while on leave or in camp in East Anglia. An Australian soldier managed to locate an uncle and, wishing to repay the old man for his hospitality, took him to London to see the zoo.

The old fellow was very interested in all the animals and eventually came to the enclosure of the kangaroo.

'What moight that be?' he asked his nephew.

'That,' replied the nephew, 'is a native of Australia.'

The uncle scratched his head.

'You don't say!' he exclaimed. 'Just imagine—I a-got a daughter married to one of them things.'

—J.R. Leader, 1330 Snowdon Street, Ottawa, Canada.

'Ain't it wunnerful that thet old zepp'lin should ha'missed Theberton an' fallen just where yew togither wanted it, roight inside thet barbed wire.'

Contributed by Mrs. G. Goddard, 67 Springfield Lane, Ipswich.

THE TWO BRASS KNOBS

A man was being shown round the church by the verger. In the chancel he noticed that the altar rails were surmounted by large brass knobs but only two of them—one on each side of the gate leading to the altar—were polished, all the others being dull.

The visitor asked the verger why all the knobs were not polished, saying that it would look much better if they were.

'Oh no, sir, no,' said the verger. 'Them two's our holy ones.'

'That's funny,' said the visitor. 'How can a brass knob be holy'? To which the verger replied:

'Well, thas like this here, sir. Two year ago the bishop he come here for a confirmation and him being a bit short-sighted, like, he confirmed them two.'

—Tom E. Matthews, The Red House, Cowfold, Sussex.

THE INVISIBLE PATIENT

My great uncle, Sir John Cordy Burrows when a doctor in Suffolk many years ago, was called to see a woman. After he was admitted to the house and had been there several minutes he said to the daughter:

'My good woman, where is your mother?'

She replied: 'Please, sir, you're a-settin' on her.'

—Mrs. E.M. Deane, Castle Acre, King's Lynn.

THE UNLABELED EVACUEE

When the evacuees arrived in an East Anglian village a kind old lady was doing her best to help at the reception centre. Suddenly she exclaimed:

'This poor little boy hasn't a label on him.'

An outraged villager replied: 'He's my child.'

—Olive Mary Oakley, 14 Albert Road, Framlingham.

WHUT HAR?

As our good friend hinder said, when darscribun a ralative: 'Whut har? Why she'd taake the last tooth outa yar hid an' bite ye with uf.'

—Phoebe Lockud, Strit Farm, Thorndun, Oi, Suffick.

WAITING TO BE LOADED

A farmer I knew 50 years ago decided to send his stockman away for a week's holiday. All arrangements were made and James was driven to the station.

The farmer left him on the platform saying that his would be the next train in. As he was crossing the station again some time later he saw to his suprise that James was still on the platform.

'Why are you still here James?' he asked.

And the reply was: 'They didn't put me in.'

—J.E. Robinson, Lyndhurst, 10 Station Road, Harleston, Norfolk.

Drawing by Frank Harrison

COMING AND GOING

My uncle, the late John Henry Sizer, J.P. of the Mill, Great Bentley, near Colchester, who died aged 94 about 10 years ago and who was for 40 years or so a magistrate on the Tendring Hundred Bench, was very fond of telling this story.

A schoolmaster at a small village school received a note one morning from the mother of one of the boys:

'My Bill ain't a-coming to school. When starting he could not go so I gave him something to go but he stuck. As soon as he has been and gone, then he'll be coming.

—E.F. Kellett, 6 Byron Road, Ealing Common, W.5.

A HIGHLY COMPLICATED BUSINESS

A townsman spent a recent holiday in Norfolk and one day met a farmer. In the course of conversation the townsman commented on the increasing prices of farm produce.

'Well, bor,' explained the farmer,'yow see 'tis loike this here. When the farmer het tew know the botanical names of the crops he grow, the Latin names of the weeds that choke 'em, the zoological names of the insects that'll eat 'em and the chemical names of the insecticides that'll kill 'em—well, bor, then somebody het tew pay.'

—J.C. Nice, 26 Leonard Road, Gloucester.

THE BAPTISM

My husband, as vicar of the parish, was called to baptise twin boys a few days old. He was given one baby and said:

'Name this child.'

A voice from the bed called:

'Which hay ye got—the dark un or the fair un?'

—Mrs. E.M. Deane, Castle Acre, King's Lynn.

THE BENEFIT OF A COUGH

I was walking through the churchyard at Lowestoft one day when I met an old lady who seemed to have a dreadful cough: I said to her:

'Oh, dear, you'll have to get rid of that cough.'

Looking at me very sternly she replied: 'I don't want to get rid of it.'

'Don't you?' I said.

'No,' she said, 'There are plenty lying here who would be glad of it.'

—H. Carpenter, 94 Greenfield Avenue, Eastfield Estate, Northampton.

THE LIGHT THAT WOULDN'T GO OUT

An elderly couple one evening paid a visit to the village inn. When they were ready to return home it was very dark and a near neighbour offered the loan of his torch. Passing the cottage next day the lender asked for it back.

'Cor,' said the old man, 'that's on the garden. Liza couldn't blow it out and I couldn't and we were afraid that 'ud set fire to the house.'

—E.C. Cooke, East View, Wickhambrook, Newmarket.

MENDING A BINDER

I had been called to a farm one harvest to attend to a faulty binder which refused to tie the sheaves and was throwing them out loose. After making the repair, watched by the farmer, I asked him to try it out. This he did and returned at the end of the round, all smiles, saying:

'I reckon tha's done the trick. I ha' bin round once and she ha' only tied one loose un.'

—T. Quadling, 'Dreemskerry', 7 St. Clare Road, Colchester.

THE WRONG SIGNATURE

A few months ago I crossed a road at Needham, near Harleston, and heard two lorry drivers abusing one another in loud voices. It seemed that there had nearly been an accident and each driver was abusing the other.

An ancient character was standing on the footpath listening to the arguement and when the lorries finally departed he said to me:

'Ui reckon the one behuind give the wrong signature—suffen o' thaat.'

—F.G.L. Crawshay, Helston, Greenway, Gerrard's Cross, Bucks.

HOW TO GET OUT OF A HOLE

Old Ted was a labourer in a Wroxham boatyard and had been instructed by his employer to dig a large hole on a piece of waste land in which to bury rubbish. Ted got busy and as the ground was soft he soon had a sizeable hole. At lunch-time he met his friend Harry who enquired how the work was progressing. Said Ted:

'Do you know, I dug that damned hole so deep I hetta gorn borrow a ladder afore I could git out on't.'

—John Parnell, Bear's Grove, Salhouse, Norwich.

PUFFING AND BLOWING

Some boys were standing in the market place of a Suffolk town. One of them was smoking (which in those days was very nearly a crime) and the bandmaster of the local Salvation Army came up to him and said:

'D'ye know, my lad, if we were meant to smoke we should have a chimney out of the top of our head.'

'Well,' replied the boy, 'if we were meant to blow grut brass instruments we should be fitted with bellows.'

—H.M. Betts, 118 Brettenham Rd., Edmonton. N.18.

THE EXTRA HOUR

When travelling by train just after the time had changed, a dear old lady remarked:

'Just look at them dear cows. Think what a lot of extra milk they will give now that they have another hour of daylight.'

—C.J. Blake, Robins' Nest, Dallinghoo, near Woodbridge.

TIDAL

Whilst walking by the sea at Bacton recently, I noticed a young man about to bathe. As he entered the water ahead of his companions he called out to them with obvious authority:

'Toide's a-coming' in'—adding 'Or a-going out. One o' the two.'

—Mrs. D. Bowman, Wymondham College, Norfolk.

ORGANISATION

A sign seen in a business office in Ipswich:

'If you can keep a level head in all this confusion you just don't understand the situation.'

INCONSIDERATE

A young land worker had to go to work very early, leaving his wife alone in the house. One morning, as soon as he had gone, his sister (who lived nearby) saw a man from the village slip into the house, so she sent for the village constable.

Constable to wife: 'Did you shrik?'

Wife: 'No sir.'

Constable: 'Then why did they send for me and thass my day off, tew.'

—George Webb, Boxford.

DIAGNOSIS

A Norfolk woman went to see her doctor. On her return her husband asked her how she had got on. She said:

'He asked to see my tongue.'

'What happened then?'

'Oh, he said it was a case of overwork.'

'That doctor's a knowing chap', replied the husband, shaking his head.

—The Rev. R.S. Crompton, 30 Stone Street, Boxford, Colchester.

THE CRITICS

One evening in a public house in a small village close to a favourite spot on the Norfolk Broads, I overheard the following conversation between an old boatman and a holiday visitor:

VISITOR: 'I expect there's not much to do with yourselves on winter evenings. Do you have television?'

BOATMAN: 'Well, some on us du watch it sometimes. But if there's nowt much on, me missus and me puts up a gud fire and has a laugh ower some of the queer people us gets here in summer.'

—R. Wells, 38 Agnew Road, Forest Hill, S.E. 23.

BETTER BUTTER

Terry Moore, aged seven, told me this one. A village school teacher said to the boy:

'It's not Bu'ur, it's BUTTER' Say "Butter".

'Butter,' repeated the boy.

'Thass be'er,' said the teacher.

—E. H. Knights, Foundry House, Harleston.

UGLY PROBLEM

The parson was told of a serious Quarrel between two neighbours. He asked if either, in their row, had called the other ugly. His informer said no.

'Oh, well then,' said the parson,'I shall soon make peace between them.'
-Miss Lily Palmer, 88 Clay Street, Soham, Ely.

GOOD HEALTH

The day nurse was walking down the men's ward with the usual 'Good morning and how are we today?'. Passing one bed she received the gloomy reply, 'Browned off, nurse.'

'For goodness sake, cheer up', she said. 'I've got four cases of pneumonia coming in today.'

One old country boy raised his head and said:
'Ah, well, That'll be a change from Lucozade.'
—V.H. Beckett, 60 Rushmere Road, Ipswich.

The following story used to be told by the late William Bloomfield, who with his brother Fred was harness-maker at Campsea Ashe.

Old George Mattin was very ill and when his son Mark was asked how his father was he replied: 'Well, bor, some days he's all roight an' another day he's bad all the week.'
—C. Woolnough, 8 Woodville Road, Ipswich.

BORN IN A BARN

I was amused when the train stopped at Saxmundham recently. Fellow passengers got out, leaving the carriage door open. This caused a porter to come along and remark:

'They ain't got no doors attom'
—F.E. Rice, 104 Christchurch Street, Ipswich.

THE LAZY WAY

A boy was sent out to scare rooks. Soon tiring of this task, the boy lay on his back by the road-side. A motorist stopped and asked the way to a certain village.

Still lying on his back with his hands under his head, the boy sleepily replied:

'Yow taike fust tun on roight' and lazily moved the toe of his boot to the right. 'Then the nixt to the left' and he twisted the toe of his boot to the left. 'Kape stroight on tell yow come to a lef' han' tun,' he said, again twisting his toe to the left. 'Thin yow're there.'

'Well,' said the motorist,'if you can tell me a lazier way to give directions I'll give you half a crown.'

The lad turned slowly over on his side.

'Shove it in my pocket,' he said.
—E.M.M. Martin, Eastwiew, Stoke Road, Clare, Suffolk.

THE UNEXPECTED

'I'm in bad trouble, George,' said Bob. 'Can you lend me five pounds? I promise faithfully I'll let you have it back within three months.'

George handed over the fiver and, to his surprise, was repaid within the time promised.

A couple of months later Bob was once again in trouble.

'I don't like asking you again, George.' he said, 'but could you lend me 10 pounds?'

'No fear, bor,' said George. 'You sucked me in larst time.'

'Whoy, I paid you back.'

'Yis, yis. That's just it, bor. I never expected you to.'
—Ernest S. Willot, Derby House, Woodbridge.

THAT'LL LARN 'EM

I was looking at a large patch of stinging nettles which flourishes in my chicken run.

'What yew want ter dew with they,' said old Jim, 'is cut 'em down three toimes a year fer foive years.'

'Will that kill them?' I asked.

'No. But that hully weaken 'em.'
—Miss Rosemary Eade, The Old Bakehouse, Whepstead, Bury St. Edmunds.

LEARNING

Essex farmer on a visit to his aged father-in-law:

'Well, marster, how dew yew fare now?'

'Why, Jack bor, I'm all right. It's just my legs. Can't make 'em walk as I'd like.'

'How old are yew now?'

'I'm turned 96.'

'Can't say as yew haven't had time to practice, can yew?'
—Gladys V.L. Nunn, 65 High Road, Orsett, Essex.

DOWN OVER

I was talking to an elderly man in our village when I suddenly caught sight of a flock of wild geese flying very high overhead. I said, 'Look up there.'

The old man turned and, glancing upwards, said:

'Coo, they're what yew call up there some depth.'

—Mrs. D. Riley, Little Saxes, Stanningfield, Bury St. Edmunds.

STARBOARD TACK

I emigrated from Ipswich 11 years go. Early this summer I was over on a visit, with my seven year old son, a Canadian who had never been to England before. We were driving out of the Butter Market one day, when I saw a car driven by a young lady about to cross the T road ahead of me. Thinking she was only a girl and would give way to me, I accelerated. Then I saw she would not, and I had to brake hard.

When we got round the corner, my young son turned to me and said:

'Daddy, Ipswich girls don't scare easy.'

—John S. Catchpole, 14515 106A Avenue, Edmonton, Alberta.

INCONSIDERATE

It used to be the custom on the approach of winter for mothers to wrap their children in flannel. This was often stiched on and not removed until the spring.

One year the school medical officer was rather late in making his inspection and one mother was heard to wail:

'That old fule doctor would ha' t' come jest when I'd sowed boy Jimma up for the winter. Now I a-got it all to undo.'

—Miss Janet Hitcham, Cropley Grove, Ousden, Nr. Newmarket.

SHORT-SIGHTED

Jack Brown was a crafty sort of chap. He went through the woods to work each day and on the way used to collect the hares from the snares he had set the night before.

One morning, as he was approaching a snare, he saw footprints in the dew. He stopped a yard short and pretended to do up a shoelace.

'Got you at last', said the keeper who had been hiding in the bracken. 'Caught you taking that snare up.'

'I was doing my lace up', said Jack. 'Good thing you told me. I can see it now. I might have tripped up if you hadn't spoke.

—T. Thompson, Heathward, Walberswick.

HOW DO YOU DO?

A country man had been ill. One morning, as he stood out by his gate, a friend came along and said 'How are you now?'

'Oh, I feel a lot better this morning,' he replied.

At that moment his wife came out and said:

'How d'yar know how yar dew? The doctor han't been yet.'

—Mrs. T. Hornaby, Little Wilbraham, Cambs.

JUST AS FAST

Many years ago, an old tramp entered a first class compartment of a train at Wisbech St. Mary station and was promptly ejected by the station-master, who pushed him into a third class compartment.

As the train drew out, the man leant out of the window, stuck his tongue out at the station-master and shouted:

'Yah! This goes as fast as that, don't it?'

—Fred Green, 435 Walnut Ave., St. Lambert, Montreal, 23, P.Q.

A QUESTION OF BEVERAGE

An old labourer was leaning idly over Beccles Bridge one summer afternoon. He was a well-known character because of his hard drinking habits.

In the shallow water of the Waveney by the side of the 'Ship Inn' the horses of the local maltster were just turning away after their usual daily drink before being stabled for the night.

At that moment the owner arrived and, noticing the old man, slapped him on the shoulder, remarking:

'There you are, ———, my horses know when they've had enough.'

Came the reply without hesitation: 'Ah, bor, so do I—if it's only water!'
—A.C. Fairweather, 51 Caxton Road, Beccles.

Based upon an anecdote from R.A. Brown, 48 Alexandra Road, Beccles.

PARENTAL AUTHORITY

FATHER TO SON: 'Bill!'
SON: 'What?'
FATHER: 'Come yow in. Thass gitten late.'
SON: 'I shorn't.'
FATHER: 'Stop where yow are, then. I wool be minded somehow.'
—J. Cook, 14, Springfield Lane, Ipswich.

TIME AND WEATHER

Two comfortable-looking country women, one with her hat anchored with an outsize hatpin, were on the bus. Said the first:

'Tha git light when it orter an' that git dark when it orter an' they didn't orter alter it.'

'Thass right!' said the second. 'They dint! An' we ain't half 'ad a rare owd winter so I reckon we'll have a rare owd summer.'
—Miss. M. Thrower, 463 Norwich Road, Ipswich.

THE HARE AND ALBERT

Among the parcels for delivery by Albert, our village postman, some years ago, was a live hare in a basket. As Albert trudged along the road the hare somehow got out and ran off across the fields.

Albert stopped, then shook his fist at the animal and bawled out:

'Ha! 'Ass no good you a-runnen 'cus you ain't got the laybel!'
—E.A.H. Ward, The Brown House, Thorpe Lea Road, Peterborough.

WE HETTA BE EXACT

A carpenter and an engineer were discussing how accurate they had to be in measuring their work.

'In our work,' said the engineer, 'we measure to within thousands of an inch.'

'We measure nearer than that,' said the carpenter. 'We hetta be exact.'

—John G. Golden, Church Street, Northrepps, Cromer.

INTELLIGENCE TEST

A school inspector visited a village school and said to a class of boys:

'I want to test your powers of observation. Will a boy please give me a number of two figures and I will write it on the blackboard.'

'Forty-nine,' one boy called out.

'Forty-nine,' repeated the inspectoı 'Thank you,' and he wrote on the blackboard 94. He waited a moment or two and as no-one spoke he said:

'Will another boy give me a number of two figures and I will write that on the board.'

'Seventy-two, sir,' said another boy.

'Thank you,' said the inspector. 'Seventy-two.' And he wrote 27 on the board. Then he turned to the class and still no one spoke and so he said:

'I don't think your powers of observation are very high but I will give you one more chance. Will another boy give me a number of two figures and I will write that on the board.'

A small boy at the back of the room shouted out:

'Firty-free, marster, and dew yew try mucking about wiv that.'

—Morgan A. Hardingham, 'Broadleigh,' Harbour Road, Oulton Broad, Lowestoft.

THE PARTICULAR PORTER

My son and his pal sat on the mantelpiece in a waiting room on the Elsenham-Thaxted line on a very cold day when there was no space left in front of the fire.

A porter passing by called out: 'Git down. That shelf worn't made for what you're a-usin' on it for.'

—E.L. Jenner, 8 New Row, Steyning, Sussex.

GRAVE OBJECTION

Old Jacob was told of the extension of the village graveyard by the acquisition of part of an adjoining field. It was suggested that Jacob would probably eventually find a resting place therein, whereupon he remarked:

'Me buried in Old Easter's field? Not likely! I'd walk to Burgh fust!'

—Mrs. K.M. Webster, 12 Lake Walk, Clacton-on-Sea.

NOT OFTEN

FIRST OLD LADY; 'Du you like ice cream, my dear?'

SECOND OLD LADY: 'Yis, I like it but I don't niver have none, not if I ain't out wi' nobody.'

—W.C. Clark, 21 King Edward Road, Ipswich.

TAKING A HINT

A clergyman taking over temporary Sunday duty asked the parish clerk to place a glass of water in the upstairs pulpit so that he could drink it before starting his sermon.

After the service the minister remarked:

'You know, John, that might have been gin for all the congregation could tell.'

On the next occasion he discovered to his horror that it was gin. Came a stage whisper from John below:

'I took the hint, sir, I took the hint!'

—G. Bloomfield, Cliff Lane, Ipswich.

NO NEED TO PINE

In a village near Hadleigh where I was born our chapel used to rely on a sort of lay preacher to take a little service on Sunday evenings. One Sunday no-one turned up and, rather than go home, the congregation decided to sing hymns of their own choosing. One old land worker, long since passed on, got up and said:

'Doan't know ta number but less hev that air one where ut saay "We oon't poin (pine) here fer wittles".' No. 426 in the Sankey hymn book.

—Mary Denny, 38 Hotson Road, Southwold.

UP THE SPOUT

There used to live in this area an old farmer who was renowned for selling watered milk. The inspectors had tried to catch him at it many times but always without success. He was too cunning for them, once even tipping the milk out on to the street to prevent a sample being taken.

At last his customers decided to do something about it. One market day a neighbour hurried up to him, apparently much concerned, and said:

'Yew wanter git orf home, bor. Yewr best cow's got a tarnup stuck in har throat.'

The old man raced home to find–a turnip stuck up the spout of his pump. *Miss R.I. Clarke, Church Farm, Bramfield, Halesworth.*

RECEPTACLE PROVIDED

My grandfather used to tell a story of a farmer which concerned an event supposed to have taken place near Woodbridge many years ago.

The farmer was driving home from market with his grown up daughter in their horse and trap. At one point of their journey they were held up by robbers who demanded their money. After searching the pair and finding nothing, the highwaymen appropriated the horse and trap and drove away, leaving the farmer and his daughter standing by the roadside.

Father and daughter looked at one another and finally he said:

'What did you do with the purse?' to which the daughter replied by producing it from her mouth and said 'You often tell me that my mouth is too wide but it's bin useful today.' Father was silent for a few minutes, then he said:

'Pity your owd Mother worn't here, we could have saved the hoss and cart.' *–R.M. Gale, Red Roofs, Hales, Norwich.*

A UTILITY WOODEN SUIT

Two very old friends met in a public house in Norwich. One was a retired market gardener and the other an undertaker.

'I'm glad to see yew, Tom,' said the retired market gardener. 'I'm wantin' yew to measure me up for a corfin.'

'What, so soon? What's the hurry?'

'No hurry at all, bor, but I'd kinda like to git one afore the price go up. What ken yew do?'

'Well,' said the undertaker,'I can make you a good un for £10.'

'Ten pown! Tha's tew pown dearer than our village carpenter'll do'n for me.'

'Maybe so,' replied the undertaker, 'but them sort o' corfins are like utility suits. Yew int in the d––– things a fortnit afore your ackymyarta is a-stickin' out a-through the bottom.'

–A. Jex, M.C., 70 Arbuty Road, Cambridge.

NOT IN SIGHT

Joe and his wife lived alone in a cottage miles from anywhere. One night, during a storm, his wife turned the looking glass towards the wall so that the lightning would not reflect on it.

In the morning, when Joe came down, as usual he went to the glass to straighten his tie but could not see anything.

He stood there for some time rubbing his eyes and finally called out:

'Hey, gal, Oi shall ha'ter goo back to bed agin. Oi in't awake as yet.'

–D.J. Gilder, Raydon Post Office, Hadleigh.

ANNUAL EVENT

Conversation in the local got round to the subject of washing.

'An' how offun du yu worsh yar feet, George?'

'Warl Bor, Oi worsh me feet once ivry year—wither thay be aneedun ut 'r no.'
—Hugh R. Chandler, The Rowans, Needham, Market.

EXERCISING HIS CHOICE

A local worthy was asked during an election for whom he was voting.

'Oh', replied the man. 'I'm going to have a change this time. I'm going to vote for a woman—Poll Early.'
—Kathleen Reeves, 14 Clarendon Road, South Woodford, E.18.

NOMINAL

Doctor writing a certificate and fishing humorously for a boy's full name from his initials:

'Ezekia!?'

BOY'S MOTHER:

'No. That's is father's name. 'is name's Ephraim.'
—Dr. H.S. Gaskell, 17 Recreation Road, Stowmarket.

NO HURRY

About 40 years ago in the Norfolk village where I lived I remember an old verger whose duties included the general tidiness of the churchyard.

One day the rector pointed to a damaged stone wall and suggested to the verger that he repair it before it got any worse. The verger replied:

'That baint' in no hurry, Parson. Them's that are in ont git out—and them's that are out bain't in no hurry to git in.'
—S. Catchpole, 106 Young Street, New Plymouth, New Zealand.

PRIMA DONNA

In bygone days, when the village concert was the highlight of the winter, a professional soprano who had come to live in the district was asked to contribute an item.

The next day, one of the audience was describing the performance to a friend who had not been there.

'Bor', he said, 'she hullered and she shruck.'
—K.M. Moaksom, Eaton House, Aldeburgh.

NO PROBLEM

A friend of mine many years ago wrote to Happisburgh for rooms, asking at the same time what the sanitary arrangements were. The reply was:

'You don't need worry about them. We hain't got none.'
—J.F.R. Buttle, Turret Cottage, Lynton, Devon.

SCARING THEM OFF

A passer-by saw that the farm hand who had been sent to the field as rook scarer was stretched out beneath the hedge, seemingly taking his time over his bread and flask of tea.

'Yew ont git far in that jorb if yew doan't buck up', he called.

Oi know 'ow far Oi got', came the reply, "'cos Oi put a stick in where Oi left orf.'
—The Rev. Douglas C. Sparkes, Torwood, 12 Wallis Road, Waterlooville, Portsmouth.

HIS USUAL SEAT

Last week our most venerable customer, aged 94, came in and walked to the bar for his usual 'pint'. He picked up his glass and, seeing someone occupying his normal seat, he said:

'Move up a bit, booy.'

The 'booy' is in his 81st year.
—Mrs. M.L. Gooch, The Crown, Acton, Sudbury.

AWASH

A village elder in south Norfolk was watching the traffic force its way through a flooded road. Then another villager came along on a bicycle and began to ride through the flood. The village elder shouted out:

'Hullo, Billa, bor. What, yew a-washing yar boike?'

—A.K. Robertson, St. Edmunds, Fair Close, Beccles, Suffolk.

Drawing by Paul Hogarth

BASHFUL

Mr. Squirrell, the carrier to Wattisham and Nedging, used to tell a story of two of his passengers, a mother and daughter, who went into a well known store near the Cornhill. The daughter had obtained a pair of fashionable stockings and wished to buy more like them but was too shy to say so.

The assistant showed her many pairs which he thought suitable but the girl only giggled and shook her head. Soon the mother's patience came to an end and she cried out:

'Good Lor', we shall miss that ow carrier. Cock ya leg over the counter and let Mr. Waterlow see what ya du want.'

—A.J. Deanes, 69 Rosehill Road, Ipswich.

SIGHTSEER

My father, a true Norfolk man who lived for many years at Wiggenhall St. Mary the Virgin, took a great interest in Norfolk people. Sorting through his papers I found the following note marked as 'from Bill F———'.

'Did I ever tell yew about my brother Jack? Like me he worn't no horseman but one day the boss said: "Jack, I want yew to take the waggen with tew hosses and go to the mill and fetch some meal."

'Well, bor, Jack han't niver druv tew hosses and when he got on the Tottenhil Rud he was so pleased with hisself that he kept on gitten out o' that there waggen to see how he looked when he was in it.'

—Miss F.J. Hignell, 53D Bateman St., Cambridge.

NOT THE CHIMNEY-SWEEPING SEASON

When we went to live in Suffolk over 30 years ago we moved into a spotlessly clean cottage just before Christmas, so our first spring-cleaning was begun a little later than is customary.

On going to the sweep's house to ask him to come and sweep our chimneys I was told that he could not do so as he was doing haysel. When I suggested that he might come on a wet day the reply was:

"No, he won't be weeeping any more chimneys. He's had his bath!'

—Douglas L. Christian, 7 West Hatch Manor, Ruislip, Middx.

THE CHRISTENING

The parents with their five-year-old boy arrived at the village church for the christening. The vicar, expecting to see an infant in arms, was rather surprised.

'And where is your infant son, Mrs. Turner?' he asked.

Mrs. Turner, pointing to her five-year-old child, replied: 'That's me boy what's got to be done, sir.'

'But aren't you, er, a little late?'

'I'm ever so sorry, sir,' said the good lady, 'but me husband had an awful job to get the car started.'

—Miss Kathleen B. Gingell, Horningsea Manor, Cambridge.

SHOOTING THE ENGLISH WAY

A dog-handler kindly invited a visiting foreigner to a shoot. Soon one of his young dogs ran into a hare and 'to larn him' the dog-handler fired a blank cartridge at the dog's stern. As the hare, with the defaulting dog, passed down the line, the foreigner drew a bead on the spaniel and killed it.

Asked why he replied:

'I saw the owner miss the dog so naturally I did my best and was lucky.'

—The Earl of Albemarle, Martlesham, Woodbridge.

THE NEXT TRAIN TO CLACTON

Quite recently I was waiting on Chelmsford Station. As a porter approached pushing a luggage truck I asked him:

'Porter! Is the next train in for Clacton-on-Sea?'

He looked thoughtful and replied: 'Two's comin'in, sir, but yours is the one that stops.'

—Leslie G. Cole, 43 Wash Lane, Clacton-on-Sea.

THE CYCLIST AND THE BULLOCK

An old Suffolk sea-skipper was describing a street accident in which a cyclist, a bus and a bullock had been involved: 'The fellow on the bike came hard down to luff under the stern of the bus and ran right 'thwart the bows of the bull and foundered.'

—A.W. Bullard, 62 Severn Road, Ipswich.

A.R.P.

During the war in Norwich the siren went in the middle of the night and an elderly couple got out of bed, as usual, to go to the shelter.

The husband went downstairs and, when his wife did not follow him, called up to her. She shouted back:

'I'm coming. I'm coming. I'm just putting on some tidy clothes. I want to look respectable when they find me.'

When they got to the shelter, an old man had just been given some ear llugs to minimise the noise of the bombs and guns. After wearing them for a few minutes he took them out saying:

'I can't get on with them thaar things. I can hear better without 'em.

—F.J. Lumkin, Sunrise, 27 Alford Grove, Sprowston, Norwich.

MATRIMONIAL STRIFE

The squire's son was the bridegroom at a wedding in a Suffolk village. There were four ushers.

Shortly afterwards, my friend's daily lady mentioned the occasion, saying:

'They tell me they 'ad four hushers at the wedding, ma'm. Thet fare funny. Surely they worn't 'spectin' a row at young squire's doo!'

—John Durrant, Great Cornard, Suffolk.

A NIGHTMARE

Two Norfolk lads at King's Lynn parted one night after a convivial evening. Next morning Bill said to his friend George:

'Co, I had a norful nightmare last night.'

'Yis bor,' said George, 'I know yow had. I saw yer out with her.'

—J.F.R. Buttle, Lynton, Devon.

TEA TIME

A passenger was travelling on a night train which stopped at a lonely junction to connect with the train from Norwich. After the train had been standing at 'the dimly lit platform for several minutes he called out from the window to an elderly porter:

'Excuse me, have I time for a cup of tea?'

'Yis, thet yew hev', answered the porter wandering off towards the engine.

The passenger searched the station for the refreshment room without success. Returning to his carriage, he met the porter again.

'I thought you said I could get a cup of tea?'

'No, bor, Oi said yew'd got time fer one. Oi never said as yew could git one.'

—M.J. Warde, Lavender Cottage, Westhorpe, Stowmarket.

TRUTHFUL

Sign seen in the office of a local firm: THIS IS A NON–PROFIT MAKING ORGANISATION, IT'S NOT THE WAY WE LIKE IT–IT'S JUST THE WAY IT IS.

UP AND DOWN

Overheard in a hotel at Oulton Broad:

'Thes a rummin how daft some blokes can be, i'nt it? Me and my mate had to go and dig a old sump hole on a farm. I was in the hole and my mate on the top chucking the muck inter a barrer.

'Dinner time come and the old hole was a-gittin' deep so I sent my mate to borrer a ladder so I could git out.

'Arter a long time he come back with no ladder. "Whas a matter". I say. "Ont old Bill let you have one?"

'He say: "He's only got one you go up on. I told him that wunt no good. We want one what you go down on."

—H.R. Hindes, 4 Queen's Road, Dovercourt.

NO FLIES ON GEORGE

George was a true man of the Norfolk soil, being known locally for his dry, uncultured wit. He had finished harvest on the Friday and next day, for the first time in his life, he made his way to London. It was customary for George to have a shave every Saturday and there he was in London with his usual week's growth of bristling beard.

His first call, obviously, had to be at the barber's and in he strolled with a 'good mornin' greeting to the proprietor and the remark:

'Kin I hev a shave, bor.'

George sat in the chair and the operation was duly performed, not without perspiration from the brow of the proprietor and tears from George.

'How much do I owe you, bor?' asked George, and received the answer, much to his disgust:

'Two shillings, if you please.'

'Tew bob!' said George, 'Cor, blarst. bor, I only pay tuppence where I come from.'

'Well, two shillings is my charge,' said the proprietor.

At that moment George gazed at the ceiling.

'Marster,' he said, 'yow a-got a rare lot o' flies on yar ceiling.'

'Yes, ' said the barber. 'It's a job to get rid of them at this time of the year.'

"'Well,' remarked George. 'I'll tell yow how to git rid o' them. You just gi' me that two bob back and I'll tell yow.'

The barber was only too pleased to repay George the two shillings to receive such information.

'Thanks, marster,' said George. 'Well yer see, yow git a-howd o' each one o' them flies, shave the b---s like yow shaved me and charge 'em two bob and they on't come iny more.'

–R.M. Neale, 62 Giffords Cross Road, Corringham, Essex.

NO REAR LIGHT

A sheperd who had his sheep folded in a nearby village had to cycle there and back each day. One evening the local policeman stopped him and said:

'You haven't got a rear light.' After some discussion he concluded: 'Go on home.'

The old shepherd had gone about 50 yards when he turned round and shouted:

'Hi! You didn't notice I hadn't got a front un, did yer.'

–G.B. Webb, Stone Street, Boxford, Suffolk.

EVEN HOMER NODS

A batsman at a village cricket match having been run out when he was half way down the pitch was given 'not out' by the umpire.

The crowd watching were very much annoyed and began shouting: 'Why worn't he out? Why worn't he out?'

The umpire, infuriated, turned to them and shouted at the top of his voice:

'Ow the 'ell can 'e be out when I worn't a-looking?'

—R. Bagnall, Hockham Lodge, Shropham, Norfolk.

FOXED

My grandfather was very fond of hunting. One morning he arrived after hounds had moved off so he went straight on to the first covert. Wishing to know if the huntsman (whose name was Bailey) and the hounds were still there, he rode up to an old man and asked him if the fox had gone away.

'No 'e ain't was the answer. 'Do Bailey 'ud a let 'em went.'

—Nancy Blyth, 44 Stortford Road, Dunmow, Essex.

GRUNDISBURGH POND

Many years ago at Grundisburgh the only water supply was from a dirty weed-covered pond. A visitor, horrified at this, asked what steps were taken to prevent an epidemic and received the reply:

'Fust of all we strains it, then we biles it, then we drinks beer.'

—C.E. Grainger, Flower Farm, Walpole St. Andrew, Wisbech.

AMATEUR

An old man in our village had a lodger who was learning to play the cornet. When I asked him how the lodger was progressing, he replied:

'He makes a row like a weanin' calf.'

—Frank Farnsworth, 261 Main Road, Broomfield, Chelmsford.

ME TOO

The Rev. E. Oakley, Vicar of Halstead, was, as was his wont, walking down the middle of the High Street in his white linen hat and accompanied by his little black dog.

He encountered one of his parishioners whom we will call John. The vicar accosted him with:

'Drunk again, John!'

And John's reply was: 'So am I, sir.'

—Harrold F. Coles, 42 Colchester Road, Halstead, Essex.